W9-BNN-605

Songs from the Black Chair

American Lives SERIES EDITOR Tobias Wolff

University of Nebraska Press LINCOLN & LONDON

Charles Barber

Songs from the Black Chair

A Memoir of Mental Interiors

W

Passages from "The Fort" appeared previously in
The Harvard Health Policy Review (Spring 2003).
The chapter "Songs from the Black Chair" ap-
peared previously in *The Bellevue Literary Review*
(Spring 2004).

Library of Congress Cataloging-in-Publication Data
Barber, Charles, 1962–
Songs from the black chair : a memoir of mental
interiors / Charles Barber.
p. cm. – (American lives)
ISBN 0-8032-1298-4 (cloth : alk. paper)
1. Barber, Charles, 1962 – Mental health.
2. Mentally ill – United States – Biography.
3. Psychiatrists – United States – Biography.
I. Title.   II. Series.
RC464.B365A3 2005
616.89'0092 – dc22
2004018191

Set in Minion by Kim Essman.
Designed by A. Shahan.
Printed by Thomson-Shore, Inc.

To Laura, for faith—first and last

contents

acknowledgments

A book on issues as difficult as these would not have been possible without the assistance and kindness of many people along the way. In particular, I would like to thank Shazaf Azim, Alex Bloom, John Burton, Rita Charon, Robert Coles, Tony Connor, Francine Cournos, John Dlugosz, Alan Felix, Rebecca Garden, Jason Gold, Sabra Goldman, the late Paul Horgan, the late J. Anthony Lukas, Duncan Marr, Wilfredo Mercado, Jonathan Parizer, Anne Pedersen, Andy Podell, Faye Radin, Ladette Randolph, Michael Rowe, Dan Sharp, Lisa Stern, and Alexi Wisher.

I want to thank Dick Ohmann for his extraordinary support and open mind. David Marchetti's irreverent spirit and loyalty have inspired a wonderful, multidecade friendship.

Three writers served as mentors at various points during the long and arduous passage of this book. Phyllis Rose provided brilliant advice and guidance at critical points, especially at the beginning when I didn't know what I was getting into. William Finnegan took an interest in me and my story when he didn't have to. He has been exceedingly generous. At the very end, Kit Reed provided a much needed boost, in the form of tea, biscotti, and writerly advice.

My brothers, Tom and John Barber, have been unendingly supportive and positive, during both the lived experiences and the documentation of it. They are remarkable. My parents have been constantly loving throughout. This book has been difficult for them, but they have understood.

Finally, both the living and the writing would simply not have been happened without the support and love of my wife, Laura Radin. Words cannot describe my debt to her. Tears of joy perhaps, but not words.

author's note

For the purposes of confidentiality,
most of the characters in this text,
as well as some institutions and places,
are identified with pseudonyms.

Henry

What people are ashamed of
usually makes a good story.
F. SCOTT FITZGERALD,
The Last Tycoon

. . . we argued about being and
nothingness and called a
certain kind of inconsequential
behavior "existentialist." . . .
We duly felt the right anguishes.
JOHN FOWLES, *The Magus*

Pale Light

This is the way I imagine that it happened:

The decision was made three days ago when he stopped eating. Decision? Well, not a decision in any pure sense of the word—nothing conscious or deliberate about it—it was more like, when he stopped eating he knew, then, that he wanted to die. It wouldn't be like before, the reckless swallowing of pills in the bathroom of his parents' home, followed by the far worse torment of weeks and then months in psychiatric units and "residential treatment centers," surrounded by goons, being forced to take Thorazine for god's sake, and being treated like a pariah, an idiot, a fool. No, this would be a quiet, well-done professional suicide. He alone would be involved. Simple. Clean. No blood. Suicide was just like anything else, he thought: the more you attempted it, the better you got at it.

It made sense, you know. Everybody had left: his father had left; his sister had left; his mother, if she had ever been there, had left long ago; girlfriends had left; his last two friends, Nick and Charlie, had left last Sunday morning as he lay hungover in bed. He retained a vague alcoholic memory of his friends mumbling something to him about going back to Cold River. Going back to Cold River, as he told them then and thought now, was not even an option. Cold River was good for only one thing—getting as drunk as possible. No, he was alone now just as he had always been alone, and it was clear to anyone observing that he was never going to get out of the tunnels he was living in; nothing, it was now eminently clear, would ever change. He wasn't stupid. He came from a family of professors in his parents' generation and of corporate executives in his grandparents' who were, at their best, entirely proficient at making sense of the world. That part of his brain that was still intact and not fouled up by LSD, *alcohol, speed, etc., could play that game too, and any* rational summing up of things pointed in the direction of stopping the production. His grandfather, the comptroller, would have agreed, surely: the numbers just didn't add up. As he lay in bed, he recalled for some reason that there had been a questionnaire in one of the hospitals. "What do you expect to be your career choice?" Suicide, he had written, in careful letters.

The house was entirely still when he got out of bed at noon. Getting up at noon, relatively speaking, was quite early; in the last month at the farm he had typically been getting up at four or five in the afternoon so as to avoid the daylight. But he planned on this day, the day, to get up really early, say nine o'clock, but that plan, too, had failed. It had seemed the appropriate thing to do, on your last day, to get up early. I mean, what the hell was he going to do, sit around all day before killing himself? Would he be cured if he waited until nightfall? Might all the scary monsters flee if he waited just one more day, so that tomorrow, on some fine new morning he would step out with a fresh attitude and become, what, a contributing member of society, a taxpayer, a citizen? Might he learn to function? Or learn to crawl? But that too had come to nought—he had been too hungover from the scotch and tequila experiments of the previous night to get up at nine.

He went downstairs. The temperature got a little colder as he descended each step of the wooden staircase. By the time he reached the bottom step he could almost see his breath. His father had never wanted to install a proper heating system. Last night's bottles were on the round kitchen table. Last night he had spent a great deal of time, very drunk, looking closely at the wood grain in various parts of the surface of the table. He had become for perhaps an hour a student of wood grain, an examiner of minute changes in color and texture. He who had once been a student of promise (high honors and all that shit) was now, happily, merely an ardent student of an oak table. It had been soothing last night to lose himself in the patterns of the table, the most fun he had had in weeks, but now in the light of day wood ceased to be interesting. It all looked the same; it was boring. No, it was boring and annoying.

What for breakfast? Or was it lunch now? Scotch or tequila? He would not mix them today. Scotch, he thought. He needed things to be clear. In the dark kitchen he filled a coffee cup halfway with scotch. He drank some and walked outside. He realized, by how cold the grass was, that it was almost November. There was a pale light on the grass and the hills, and the grass itself was almost white from a dusting of frost. Everything outside was as still as in the house. Looking down he noticed he was wearing no shoes or socks, but it didn't matter, he liked the sensation of his naked feet on the cold of the grass. He saw too that he was wearing nothing but black jeans, no shirt, and that the jeans smelled of sweat and urine because he had worn them for four days straight. He thought of the many people, particularly the women he had known, who would have thought that was disgusting, thought that he with his urine and sweat was disgusting. He didn't think he was disgusting. His belly was flat from the three days of not eating. He put his hand on it and felt its flatness with some satisfaction. Funny that he should care.

He walked over the patch of lawn in front of the farmhouse. He walked to the brown pond. Not a ripple on it. Flat. Without motion. Beyond the pond he saw the first line of naked trees, followed by more trees, followed by hundreds and thousands and maybe even millions of more naked trees, covering the miles and miles of almost completely uninhabited hills that went down to the valley, where the towns and colleges and bars and auto-parts stores were, along with everything else human. The trees, he thought, were like waves of soldiers, wave after wave of an oncoming army, one after the other after the other. If you mowed down the first row, there'd always be another one to follow. He thought maybe what had happened in his life, all that had really happened, was that he had been involved in a war with the trees, and however hard he tried, there were so many more of them than there were of him, and they had been swarming him for years, and they were swarming him now. He was losing—or, actually, had lost—the war with the trees. He noticed that the leaves had all fallen off them now. The leaves covered the ground everywhere in splotches. The leaves were fading, becoming more gray and brown each day, losing their color and shape and becoming inexorably part of the earth. They were half leaf and half earth now, he thought.

"Inert," he said, holding the coffee cup with only his black jeans on. "The leaves are inert. In-ert. In earth," he said out loud.

The scotch had been a good choice. His mind was clear. If it weren't for some nausea he'd be feeling pretty good. He stood by the pond for a while longer. He felt his toes getting cold. He looked down at the coffee cup and realized he had drunk all the scotch. For no reason in particular *he said "inert" again, this time loudly, and wondered whether anybody could hear. "Inert!" he cried again to the valley. Maybe his father would hear two hundred miles away and come up the driveway in a few minutes and say, with his usual equanimity, "Hello, Henry, how are you today?" Maybe his friends, Charlie and Nick, would roll up the driveway in the white Ford Maverick, get out and say, "What's going on, man? How are you today? How do you feel?" ("Great," he would reply.) But none of that happened. He looked down again at the flatness of his belly and walked back inside the house.*

He went now to the desk in the living room and pulled from the upper right drawer two large sealed envelopes. He opened them and laid out the documents: Aetna Automobile Insurance, Policy #A133274-8192B. Name of insured: Henry Court. Age of driver: 21. Vehicle: 1977 Dark Blue Ford Econoline Van. The insured driver's record: numerous speeding tickets, one accident while driving a motorcycle, one failure to inspect. Then, Life Insurance, Policy #B00-173-2169-230. Recipients, at 50 percent each, of $300,000: William and Joyce Court, parents of Henry Court. He unfolded the papers carefully. The life insurance, he knew, was pointless. The other day he had read the fine print and found the expected words: "No liability to insurance provider in the event of death caused by self-harm." But at least his father wouldn't have to hunt for the papers to read those words himself. He would be compassionate to the end.

He had been considering the appropriate music for days. The day before yesterday he thought it was (couldn't remember exactly, it was all fuzzy), he'd listened to dozens of records, looking for the appropriate punk anthem, looking for some piece of music that said it all, or at least something. He had settled finally on an album called "Songs from the Big Chair," by the band Tears for Fears, which he realized was perhaps not the ultimate music for a final statement, perhaps not in the best of taste (Faure's Requiem, for instance, would be more to his parents' approval), but he felt that there was something perfect about the music, perhaps something about the way it was simple, absurd, and terrifying all at the same time. The cassette was waiting for him, all cued up, in the dashboard tape player in the van.

On second thought, tequila might be best. Tequila he knew best; with tequila he could handle the pill and not fuck things up. "Inert!" he cried again to the valley. "Inert!!" For about five minutes he sipped the tequila directly from the bottle, and he thought: this will be the last thing I will ever taste. Then he held the pill and thought, no, maybe the pill will be the last thing I will ever taste. But as he swallowed it, he couldn't quite taste the pill; there was just the slightest flutter of bitterness as he felt it going down his throat, and so he thought, this time finally and deliberately and with great certainty, that in fact it would be the tequila that would be the last thing he would ever taste.

He felt an odd nervousness but also, he believed, an odd calmness as he walked out of the farmhouse and onto the frosted grass. He could see his breath. He shut the front door of the house firmly behind him. He felt better being outside. He breathed. He looked at the pond again, and the trees. He felt nervous and happy. He walked to the van.

It was later estimated to be about two p.m. on October 21 that he started the van's engine, shut the door, pushed "play" on the cassette player, sighed, and looked for a final time at his handsome, intelligent, barely lined face. The meticulousness with which he had attached the vacuum cleaner tube to the exhaust pipe and then rerouted it back into the van was totally worth it. It was amazing how quickly the noxious fumes filled his lungs.

◈ ◈ ◈

But the only thing I know for sure is that my friend Henry Court killed himself, by asphyxiating himself in his van, while listening to the album *Songs from the Big Chair* by the middling British band Tears for Fears, in the driveway of his parents' vacation house in the Berkshires, sometime on the day of October 21, 1983, and that alcohol and some type of narcotic were later detected in his body.

one

Faceless

I am writing this eighteen years later. I am writing this in the evening, in the fresh coolness of a late winter night, and in the relative peace and comfort of my office in lower Manhattan. There are soothing pictures on the wall—scenes of the Adirondacks, Chagall prints, Matisse cutouts. The tragedies of youth seem far away.

On a recent drive to Cold River, the smallish New England town that Henry and I grew up in, I thought suddenly, for some unaccountable reason, of the author John Cheever. I remembered that as a lanky teenager I watched in the cool basement of my parents' home a Dick Cavett television interview with Cheever. The elderly author said that when he was in his twenties, he would have to run to the shower as fast as he could after waking each morning. "If I got there quickly enough, I knew I wouldn't commit suicide that day," he said. Cheever's words shocked and confused me at the time. I couldn't understand how anyone, particularly someone as talented and debonair as Cheever, could ever feel that way. How unbelievably wretched he must have felt! But then, just a few years later, I learned that people do feel like killing themselves, sometimes on a daily basis. The state of mind that Cheever described became something I came to understand all too well.

But these days, I thought with a warm satisfaction, things are different. As I drove on to Cold River I realized that Cheever's words once again have the power to shock and upset me. I can't quite understand them. These days I am married, with a house in the leafy suburbs of New York City, a golden retriever named Harper, and currently $112 in the pocket of my Brooks Brothers pinstripe shirt. Next week I have an appointment with my dermatologist, and the week after that with my urologist. I am concerned about the thinning hair on the crown of my head. I attend most of my sessions with my analyst. I floss regularly. My use of alcohol is moderate. I go to sleep at exactly the same time every night. I have money in the stock market—every month, I call an 800 phone number to track how my pension funds are doing. I return all phone calls promptly. My credit rating has improved dramatically. Computers all over America retain information on me that attests to my bill-paying character. I now know what the Dow Jones is. People ask me for advice on their relationships, their money, and what they should do with their lives. I am the supervisor of twenty-five people. Sometimes, as I drive across the George Washington Bridge in my Volvo every morning with the thousands of other commuters, I think that I am the conventional asshole that Henry would surely have predicted I would become.

And yet my life is not so comfortable. My Brooks Brothers shirt is wrinkled and worn through in a couple of spots; the $112 in my pocket is probably owed to somebody else. My Volvo is ten years old; if it breaks down one more time I won't be able to afford to fix it. My splendid office is actually situated at Bellevue, in the largest homeless shelter in New York City. In the floors above me, eight hundred men live on bunk beds in dozens of barracks-style rooms. At any time as I write this I may be interrupted by my clients—a long line of men with such diseases as bipolar disorder, schizophrenia, major depression, and personality disorder. They may knock on my door to speak about the voices in their heads that plague them, about their sleepless pacing nights, about their childhood sexual abuse, about the people who slip under their door, steal their stuff, and watch them in the shower. Or they may ask me to administer their medications, beautiful lovely soothing peach- and cream- and mint-colored oval and oblong and circular tablets designed to knock out their nonrealities, their disorderly unacceptable moods, their histrionic and tumultuous characters. Day after day, night after night, a long steady line of desperate men come and sit in the black chair next to my desk and quite openly tell me of their travails—prison, hepatitis, AIDS, heroin, crack, methadone, PCP, sexual abuse, mental retardation, and the voices, always the voices. Bits and pieces of this long trail of invisible men—the rhythms with which they say things, their beat-up clothes, their desperate stories, their irreverence, their obvious pain—remind me of Henry.

But it's funny. I have come to love it here. I have worked in this office for three years, and it has become a kind of home. In fact, I can't get enough of shelters. I work at two of them for a total of thirteen hours a day. During the day, I work uptown in a former armory that is now home to two hundred men with psychotic illnesses (as such, its literature proudly proclaims, it is the largest "mental health" shelter in the world), and then I get in my car, drive the length of Manhattan—which seems positively sedate and serene, a nice country town in comparison to my places of employment—and come here, to Bellevue, to work the night shift, seven to midnight. I put in these horrendous hours partially because I have to (working with the homeless mentally ill, I have come to learn, is unfortunately not exactly a lucrative calling), but mainly I do it because I want to. I feel drawn to it. My wife, who understands my odd compulsions, puts up with my hours without complaint. I get home to the suburbs at one in the morning feeling entirely depleted but deeply exhilarated. I feel cleansed and empty; I look back on the day and think that I have availed myself of something today, or acquitted myself of something. What that is, though, I do not know.

At night, between client visits, the shelter is oddly quiet. I have come to call my office the "psychotic library" for its unique atmosphere of bookish tranquillity interrupted by the periodic visits of a crazy person. Largely because of the city's newly draconian policies toward homeless services, it is harder and harder to get into the shelter system, and the long line of desperate men has thinned in recent months. So I sit here quietly and write. The occasional rat that dashes through the office doesn't bother me. Nor does the peeling paint, the single fluorescent light, the periodic floods, the indescribable odor, or the dusty fax machine that hasn't worked for five years. In fact, I am grateful to be inside this place. I love the stories, the improbable and voluminous and twisted narratives that pour out of the men within minutes of their taking a seat in the black chair, a simple ugly black metal chair, that sits next to my desk.

But above all I have come to love this place because this is the place where I have been able to write about Henry. I don't know why exactly—perhaps it has something to do with the decayed ambience, and a certain desolateness that is deeply embedded in this office that Henry surely would have approved of—but this is the place where I have been able to think and write clearly about him. And maybe, just maybe—I hope—get rid of him.

⋄ ⋄ ⋄

I'm not supposed to be here.

At night when I drive home from the shelter, I often think that I am not who I am supposed to be. I should, it seems, be nowhere near ugly black chairs that insane people come and sit in. Who knows where exactly the sons of Andover and Harvard are supposed to be, but surely it is not alone at night in a homeless shelter in a forgotten and dismal area of Manhattan. My parents look at me with a sort of blank incomprehension—a sort of embarrassed half smile invariably appears on their faces—when I tell them the stories of the people who sit in the black chair. It is not my words that they do not understand but my motivation for saying them. They believe that what I am doing is somehow not in keeping with my background, rearing, and temperament. I should be teaching philosophy or English literature at some college somewhere and writing small but terribly worthy books. I should be like my resolutely prosperous brothers—one of whom is the medical director of a large hospital, while the other has made a fortune in investment banking. I do not stay in touch with a single one of my peers from Andover and Harvard, but I read of their activities in the back pages of the alumni magazines. None of my old friends, it seems, conduct their lives in a manner that brings them anywhere near black chairs: they (or at least those who write about themselves in the class notes) all seem to be living exuberantly happy lives and pursuing wonderfully stimulating (read: lucrative) professions. I noticed recently that one such prodigiously flourishing person, a classmate of mine—and back then a rather insipid, tepid person—recently donated $250,000 to our old school.

About a year ago, on my drive home, I realized suddenly that it was Henry, in his own slovenly and desultory way, who had led me to these places. It was Henry, coupled with my own obsessive tendencies, the dark details of which I will confess later, who led me to the black chair; it was Henry who drove me away from Cold River and into the mentally subterranean worlds of Manhattan which I currently inhabit; and it was Henry who led me to Luke and Seth and Michael Jasny. But more on all that later.

For now, all I know is this: if Henry knew he was at least partially responsible for my present situation, how he would laugh, and laugh, and laugh.

❖ ❖ ❖

I can no longer see his face.

I see his body perfectly, his size and height identical to mine, with a sort of burly lankiness. I can see his clothes exactly, his punkish black leather jacket and black jeans and flannel shirt and work boots; and I can even see his lurid orange spiky hair. I see the equally lurid orange jumpsuit he used to wear when he destroyed all the things in his room. But his face—the features and contours of his eyes, nose, and mouth, their texture and shape—remains elusive to me.

In the great stories I read, those by Cheever and F. Scott Fitzgerald and Flannery O'Connor and Raymond Carver and P. D. James, there is always fairly early in the narrative a telling detail about the character's face, a precise description of some defined quality that is illustrative of inner character. I feel I should be able to exactly exquisitely describe his face; I feel I should be able to render movingly and acutely what Henry looked like. But to no avail: there's just a gray cloud where his face used to be.

❖ ❖ ❖

But hold on—maybe I can see his face after all. Maybe Henry's sitting right in front of me.

The other night at the shelter, a young white kid, probably in his early twenties, came in. I could tell in a moment that he was manic—he had wild, darting eyes; he said the words "how are you?" to me in a single rush of sound; he looked ready to explode. It was an effort for him to keep from jumping out of the chair. He did a kind of dance in the chair, swinging his arms, tapping his feet, his body swaying to a music I couldn't hear. But none of that struck me. I've seen it many times. What struck me was that he looked like Henry—the same pale face, sharp vulnerable features, spiky hair. He wore the same clothes, the same bohemian, pseudo-working-class garb: work boots, black jeans, leather jacket, T-shirt. And so all of a sudden Henry's face came back to me.

"My name's Jimmy," he said. I wanted to correct him but didn't.

Hi, Henry, I said to myself. What have you been doing for the last seventeen years?

I have a script that I follow, generally, as I interview the people who sit in the black chair. The first question I ask is: "So where have you been staying the last four weeks?" I've learned that you can tell a lot about people from where they've been staying for the last month.

"So where have you been staying the last four weeks?" I said.

"Oh, a place called Cold River. It's a small town. You wouldn't have heard of it," Jimmy said.

Cold River: I couldn't believe it. What were the chances? Wouldn't have heard of it? Cold River? It's only the place I know best in the world; the place that, if I close my eyes, I can see every inch of; the town that I love and hate in equal measure; a place that I feel fortunate I was able to escape from.

"I stayed at the mental hospital there for a while, then they let me go," Jimmy said. "I hung out on the streets for a while, then some kids at Wilson, that's the college in Cold River, took me in. I stayed in the dorms for a while, then I came to New York."

I know those dorms well, I thought. My father and Henry's father both taught at Wilson, and Henry had lived in those dorms during the brief time he was a student there. I could just envision the scenario: some artsy Wilson students happened on Jimmy, whom they considered this wild, manic, entertaining child, then adopted him for a while because it seemed fun and romantic and adventurous and an interesting sort of live sociological experiment, snuck him food from the cafeteria, let him sleep on the floor, showed him off to their friends, and then the first time that his mental illness surfaced and he became strange and overly energetic and edgy, they tired of his antics and promptly kicked him out. Just like the Wilson administration did with Henry.

"I've been everywhere, man," he said. "Maine, Providence, Boston.

I travel everywhere, looking for help. But no one helps me. Can you help me?"

"I don't know," I said.

"You know who helps me?"

"Who?" I said.

He didn't answer. He stood up abruptly. "I know what you're gonna ask me. You're going to ask me if I'm a danger to myself or others," he said. "No, I'm not a fucking danger to myself or others."

He parroted the answers I wanted to hear back to me:

"Will I take my medications? Yes, I'll take my fucking medications. Do I feel like I need to go to the hospital? No, I don't feel like I need to go to the hospital. Am I crazy but safe? Yes, I am crazy but safe."

He stood up, produced a bottle of Depakote from his pocket, and quickly swallowed three pills in front of me. "No, man, I'm safe. I'm not a threat to you or anybody else. You know what, man? I've left the quadrant of violence."

"The what?" I said.

"The quadrant of violence," he said, sitting back down. "I used to be in the quadrant of violence—used to fight when I needed to, knew how to use a knife if I had to, but I don't do that no more. It's not the way. I learned that, you see."

"I see," I said.

He jumped out of his seat again. "I'm in search of something. America, I think. I came to New York to panhandle. New York's the best place to panhandle. I can make $20 an hour in the Port Authority. It's my business, I'm a professional at it. They can see I'm well bred, that I wear casual clothes, that I'm very respectful. I'm gonna get some money together and then I'm gonna go out on the road. Go out west, California, all that shit. I'm a travelin' man, dude."

I convinced him to stay in the shelter. I referred him upstairs to the "reception center," a small psychiatric shelter for forty-five people like Jimmy. The intake worker groaned when I mentioned his name. "Oh, we know him well. He's been through here a couple of times before. Is he manic?"

"Yes," I said.

We walked upstairs to the dormitory space. "Have you been there before?" I asked Jimmy.

"I don't know," he said. "Maybe. It all kind of blends together."

I directed him to the night nurse and the dorm room.

"Many thanks, man," he said. I found him, like most psychotic people, to be entirely agreeable.

He's a lot like Henry, I thought, the same restless traveling, the same search for something, somewhere, that might make him better. But there was a difference. Henry never left the quadrant of violence.

❖ ❖ ❖

One of my few enduring talents is to block out whatever is unpleasant. Over the years I have cultivated to an art form my ability to avoid things. When I don't want to think of something, I simply don't. Well, I touch on the unpleasant thing for perhaps a second or two, and then immediately divert my mind to something inconsequential and soothing, like the football scores or the crossword puzzle.

With regard to Henry, this strategy has served me beautifully. For seventeen years I succeeded at blocking him out entirely.

If I happened on a place or memory associated with Henry . . . say, if I drove past the shacklike house where we once lived together, or came on the seedy bars that we slummed in, or passed by the cemetery where we used to drink — and where he is now buried — I would contemplate the image, the thought, the idea of a Henry for perhaps a second, and then banish him immediately. In this way I almost completely succeeded at not thinking about Henry. If I were to total up the entire amount of time I contemplated Henry's life, it would come to about five minutes, a few seconds at a time.

But about a year ago, for reasons that are still not entirely clear to me, my ability to escape Henry suddenly failed. It was, not surprisingly, in my dreams that Henry returned:

On a Sunday morning, in the suburbs of a prosperous midwestern city, I am walking through a neighborhood I am unfamiliar with. It has just rained, and the streets are clean and wet. I walk past a staid, rather boring-looking church. It is so suburban-looking that it is covered with vinyl siding. The doors are open, and I can hear the preacher's words. For some reason I am drawn to enter the church and stand in the back. The service seems to be drawing to a close.

"And now," says the minister, "please join us for doughnuts and coffee in the basement."

A well-dressed, formidable woman in the congregation stands up. "Aren't you forgetting something?" I recognize her vaguely as a distorted version of Henry's sister.

"Oh yes, oh yes," says the minister, momentarily harried. "I would be remiss if I didn't mention that today is the fifteenth anniversary of the death of a former member of our congregation, a . . . uh . . . a . . . Mr. Henry Court." This announcement is met with an impatient silence from the congregation. "And so if any of you have words of condolence for the memory of Henry and for his sister, please speak up."

Nobody moves. Finally, a graying man in a suit rises. "I believe it was in a most unchristian manner that Henry died, and I'm not sure that we should acknowledge and honor his memory in this or any other manner," he says and sits down.

"All I know is that he stole from my store and was an addict," says another man.

(A woman stands up and addresses the well-dressed woman who seems to me to be Henry's sister, or a version of her. "I don't mean to show disrespect to Louise, but . . . Henry Court molested my daughter." She says the last five words in an angry rush, as one word . . . Henry Courtmolestedmydaughter . . . HenryCourtmolestedmydaughter . . . HenryCourtmolestedmydaughter . . . There are gasps from the collective group.

I think: none of this is true. Henry was crazy, and he was an addict, but he didn't steal or rape. This is all made up. I am about to stand up to defend Henry, but his sister beats me to it.

She pauses, searching for the right words. "I know that Henry, in life, did not acquit himself well at times," she declaims, "but you must remember he was in a great deal of pain for a long, long time. I don't believe he intended any of the harm he may have caused. Let us try to remember him in a generous-spirited way."

I am just about to defend my friend when the minister nervously intervenes. "There are doughnuts and coffee, friends. Please, let us adjourn to the basement."

I leave the church, having said nothing.

Ever since I ran track and cross-country in high school, I have had recurrent dreams in which I am running through a forest or a park, getting scraped by branches and moving past rocks and streams. I am in urgent pursuit of something, the object of which is never clear. I have to get somewhere by sometime, deliver something to somebody. There is always some enormous pressure that I can't quite grasp. For years I have been running alone in these dreams. But one night Henry appeared in them. He was not actually running with me but looking down ethereally from a few feet above. He smiled at me and hovered. Characteristically, he was of no use in my rush to complete my mission, but he didn't impede me either. He was simply there, as he was in life, in abstract accompaniment. I remembered, upon waking, that when I was a member of the track team, Henry was the manager, in which role he set up the equipment and timed the runners. I was a good runner, good at the mile run especially, and I won my fair share of races. Henry had timed me as I broke the string at the finish line. I realized he had returned to his old vocation as the timer and observer of runners.

Every night for a month Henry appeared in either the church dream or the running dreams. There were other variations—in one, there was a burial after the church service. Only his parents and sister and I were at the burial, but they couldn't see me. In another version, there was a reception at the parish house, after which his sister seduced me. I found all the dreams disturbing and woke up each morning feeling unsettled.

My parents still live in Cold River, and last summer I found myself visiting them more often than I had in years. I resolved that it was time to deal with Henry's legacy. Who knows why exactly—perhaps because enough time had passed, or perhaps because I simply wanted to exorcise Henry from my newly disturbed sleep—but I found myself in my waking hours actually seeking out memories of him. When I drove past the slovenly broken-down house on the edge of the campus that Henry and I briefly shared for a particularly miserable six-month segment of our lives, I found that I no longer accelerated past it. Instead, I slowed down to examine its sagging roof and rotted-out porch. I walked around the Wilson campus, where both my father and

Henry's parents had been professors. I walked in the same circles that Henry and I used to walk in. I found myself going to the bars in the dingy parts of Cold River, where Henry and I drank pitchers of Rolling Rock beer and talked for hours about who played bass on what record. I found myself driving to the condominium development where Henry lived for a time with his parents. Evaluating the rows of geometrically identical homes, I tried to determine which one the Courts had lived in. I went to the high school track where Henry had timed me and the other runners. In my old bedroom I tried to find pictures of Henry. The only image was in our freshman yearbook, the official portrait of the track team in which a sea of adolescent faces stare directly, with "game face" on, at the camera. Of the entire team it is only Henry and I who are not looking directly at the photographer. Both of us, four rows apart, are fixated on something outside the picture, to the left. Apparently we had both found something more interesting to look at, outside the frame.

I called Nick, whom I hadn't spoken to for years. In high school, Nick and Henry and I were an irreverent trio. We had attended the local Catholic high school together, at least until junior year, when I followed my brothers to the more rarefied environment of Andover. St. Joseph's was an all-boys' school with a good academic reputation and a terrific athletic one. The football team perennially won the state championship. The track team that Henry and I served on had won something like 150 meets in a row. The school's motto, carved in black marble inside the glass-walled entrance foyer, was "Be a Man." In the midst of this competitive atmosphere, Nick and Henry and I were misfits, but we were quiet, introverted, and respectful misfits who didn't get into trouble. Our rebellion was strictly internal. We got top grades and didn't bother anybody. We each kept either to ourself or to our little pack of three. We made only rare forays into the larger social world of high school. I remember that the three of us would appear at high school dances at the girls' high school down the road and then leave after five minutes of awkwardness to go back to Henry's house and listen to the Clash and the Rolling Stones. That was far less stressful.

We were joined at times by a fourth member, Sam, another Wilson faculty brat. Henry, Sam, and I were the only Wilson kids in our class at St. Joe's, which gave us an invisible bond, whatever our individual differences. I always thought of Sam as the opposite of Henry. In fact, there was occasional friction between them: Sam was annoyed by Henry's lassitude and general state of torpor, while Henry (and Nick, too) found Sam too smooth, too socially at ease, to be genuine. In short, they doubted his authenticity. Sam was, and still is, imbued with a kind of permanent joie de vivre, which exhibited itself then primarily in prowess at sports and, if not a complete indifference, then a sort of arrogance toward bourgeois social convention. This he certainly got from his father, Tom Blake, who was both eccentric and charismatic in his role as poet in residence at the college. After sophomore year, Sam dropped out and then completed high school in the Himalayas, of all places, where a friend of his father's taught English.

Unlike our more driven and conventional classmates, who wanted to become engineers or go "into business," Sam, Henry, Nick, and I had no idea what we wanted to do with ourselves in the future, but if pressed, I think we all would have said we hoped to do something vaguely "artistic." What that meant exactly we didn't know. (Except for Nick, who had ambitions to be a well-known writer or journalist. I remember him as a sophomore saying that one day he wanted to write a column for *Time* magazine.) It didn't matter that we didn't have a plan. An idea was enough. Even in high school, Henry and I especially lived almost entirely in our heads. Picking up on our parents' intellectualism, we believed ideas were more interesting than reality, or to put it another way, that thinking something made it so. Henry in particular seemed to reside in a permanent state of abstraction. I recall that six months before he died I came across a notebook of his drawings and notes. They were filled with theories and codes, unintelligible to me but structured enough that there seemed to be some kind of system or organizing theme behind them. They were nonsensical to me, but I suspected very real to him—filled in fact with more meaning, even if psychotic, than I ever culled from our abbreviated, miserable attempts at actually speaking to each other.

The friendship between Nick, Henry, and I was, I think, one of those rare triumvirate friendships that actually worked, perhaps because we just didn't care enough about jealousies if one of us was suddenly left out. We were indifferent to rivalry. Of the three of us, Nick was the only one who consistently excelled. Brilliantly creative, he was driven in a way that Henry and I, privileged faculty brats, were not. His grandparents had arrived in Cold River after emigrating from Sicily. His father was a factory machinist, and his mother assembled thermometers in a factory. In high school at least, Nick was driven to get away from all that. Both Nick and Henry went on to Wilson after graduating from high school. For Henry, admission to college had been pro forma, since both his parents were important members of the faculty. I doubt if he would have been admitted on his own merits. Nick had no such cachet, but didn't need one. Except for one religion course in his sophomore year, he received nothing less than straight As during his entire high school career, and he was to repeat this feat in college, graduating Phi Beta Kappa and summa cum laude. Nick was brilliant, smarter, I always thought, than Henry and me put together.

When I called, Nick answered the phone on the first ring.

Nick and I had never bothered much with small talk. I got right to the point. "I want to talk to you about Henry," I said. It didn't matter that we hadn't spoken in years.

"And just why in hell would you want to do that?" Nick said, sounding annoyed. "Why would you want to write about that motherfucker?"

I was hard-pressed to give him an answer.

We didn't talk for long but set a time to get together.

◦ ◦ ◦

A few days later I visited Nick in his parents' ranch house outside Cold River, where he had lived for the last twenty years in the basement. His "lair," he called it. Nick had gained a lot of weight. He was still handsome in his rugged Sicilian way, but he had a heaviness under his eyes I had never seen before. But I was relieved to find that he retained his sarcastic, edgy sense of humor, which, as I have gotten older, I have come to think of as a cover for an immense sensitivity, or more specifically, an immense sadness.

Nick made a fire, and we drank beer in the lair. Nick now seemed willing enough to talk, and we set about trying to find things by which we could remember Henry. Nick looked unsuccessfully for a tape of Henry speaking, a tape that he was sure that he had somewhere, some stream-of-consciousness drunken narrative that Nick had recorded surreptitiously. He couldn't find it. We looked for photographs of Henry, particularly those from the last weekend we had spent with him at the farmhouse. Nick produced lots of pictures of the lonely farmhouse and the woods around it, as well as photos of Nick and me during that awful weekend, but there were absolutely none of Henry. We were puzzled. What had happened to the pictures of Henry?

"Don't you remember?" Nick said suddenly. "He wouldn't let me take his picture. Every time I brought out the camera, he ran out of the room."

I couldn't remember.

"Here." Nick showed me a picture of a dark wooden table with a bottle of tequila and a box of cornflakes on it. "I tried to sneak up on him. He was sitting at the table. But he bolted as soon as he saw the camera . . . He's right here," Nick said, pointing to a spot just outside the picture frame.

We spent the rest of the afternoon remembering Henry. It was strange—what I remembered, Nick didn't; what I didn't remember, he did. When I remembered what we said, Nick remembered an image; and when I remembered visual things, Nick recalled verbal things. I was astonished at the precision of Nick's memory. He remembered the last line Henry ever said to us: "Because every time I think about going back to Cold River, I just want to get drunk." Together in the lair that afternoon we were able to piece together most of what happened that last weekend.

"You know, I'm thinking of writing about Henry," I said.

"I've thought about doing that myself," Nick said. "If I ever wrote anything about him, I'm pretty sure I'd call it *A Bad Year for Squirrels*."

"How come?" I said, laughing.

"I remember during our freshman year at Wilson Henry and I were walking around the campus. We came across one dead squirrel in the road, and then another. About a mile later, we found a third. We said nothing, just kept on walking. About five minutes later Henry says, 'Jeez, it must have been a bad year for squirrels,' in that dry way of his."

"That was Henry," I said.

<ô· ·ô· ·ô·

The next day I looked up Mary in the phone book. Mary had been the most popular waitress at the restaurant where Henry and I worked together for a summer as dishwashers. I shouldn't really use the word "friend"; a few years older than us, she was socially in a higher and more exclusive circle than we were. But she took pity on Henry, apparently, because she agreed to be his girlfriend, at least for a week. He lost his virginity to her. She was now an elementary schoolteacher at an expensive private school in Cold River.

"Mary, do you have any pictures of Henry?" I asked.

"I think so," she said. "During the week we were together"—she laughed—"we went to a wedding. Remember? Andy the bartender got married, and there was a group portrait of everybody. Hold on a sec, let me see if I can find it." She returned in a minute. "You know, I don't see him . . . Everybody at the wedding is in the picture, except for him. He must have run away from the camera. Typical fucking Henry!" she said.

꘎ ꘎ ꘎

The last step, predictably, was to visit Henry's grave. I hadn't been there since the funeral. Henry Court is buried in the oldest cemetery and on the tallest hill in town—it must be thirty acres all told, thirty acres of stately fir trees presiding over thousands of gravestones and mausoleums. The cemetery was supposed to be an old Indian burial ground, a claim later disproved. Henry and I spent many nights on top of one particular mausoleum drinking beer and looking at the lights of the town below. On an almost apocalyptically hot and humid day last July, I drove ever so slowly into the cemetery. My dog, Harper, was in the front seat, panting resolutely despite the air conditioning. I pulled over where I knew the grave would be. It would only take a minute; I didn't plan to be maudlin. I got out of the car into the thick unmoving air. It was so humid as to be almost misty. The only sound was the chatter of automatic sprinklers scattered on the hillside.

I remembered distinctly that Henry's grave was in the corner closest to the Dunkin' Donuts. This fact had always provided me with a peculiar sense of comfort, perhaps because Henry and I also spent great amounts of time there (sobering up after the drinking), but mainly because Dunkin' Donuts, with its lurid colors and obscenely synthetic food products—in short, its overall poor taste—was something that

Henry would have appreciated being in close proximity to his final resting place. Henry's grave, I remembered, was small and modest, a piece of stone sunk flat into the ground. I inspected a number of that description, with names foreign to me—Klein, Duncan, Reynolds, Marchese, Wingdale, Hubbard—but no Court. I looked over at the Dunkin' Donuts to reorient myself. Yes, I was in the right corner, on the outer edge. I walked in circles for ten minutes.

Had Henry's grave just disappeared? Was my memory entirely fictitious? Did any of this really happen? Exasperated, I called Nick from a pay phone. I was wet from the humidity.

"You know, the same fucking thing happened to me," Nick said. "I remembered that it was in the corner nearest the Dunkin' Donuts and I spent fifteen minutes walking around looking for it. Then it occurred to me—Henry's grave is no longer on the edge. It's surrounded by newer generations of graves. It's surrounded by like fifty stones. It's in the middle of the plot now."

"Of course," I said.

"Of all things, you don't expect graveyards to change," Nick said. "But they do."

I returned to the cemetery. I drove to the same spot, walked thirty rows in, and immediately came on Henry's stone. It was even smaller than I recalled, just a simple flat two-foot-by-one-foot piece of granite, sunk directly into the earth and reading:

HENRY STEARNS COURT

Loving Son and Brother

September 27, 1962–October 21, 1983

And next to it, on an identical stone:

JOYCE STEARNS COURT

Loving Wife and Mother

November 23, 1928–October 4, 1989

Christ, I'd almost forgotten about his mother. Another example of my ability to suppress the unpleasant, I thought. I looked at the dates and thought: yes, it was almost exactly six years later that she died. She lasted six more years, and then she followed him down the same path. She had always been shaky since I'd known her, a house ready to fall at any time, but she hit new agonies after Henry died. I remembered her drunken phone calls to my mother. His suicide did kill her off, I thought. It wasn't a murder-suicide but a suicide-murder, or to be more precise, a suicide-matricide.

Poor Joyce Court. She had once been a brilliant scholar, writing books and articles about Virginia Woolf and Ford Madox Ford and doing feminist literary work twenty years before it became fashionable. At the same time she excelled at managing her family's money, much of which had been inherited from her industrialist father, reading the *Wall Street Journal* at breakfast each morning and calling her broker to make changes in her portfolio. I remembered what a colleague of hers said after Joyce died, "I have never seen anyone go to the dogs as fully and completely as Joyce Court."

I stood at the graves for about five minutes, while Harper paced in the backseat of the car. I thought about what remained of Henry, and his mother, in the coffins that lay five feet below my feet. After fifteen years, would the bones have started their decay into pieces of dust? How long do skeletons stay intact? A hundred years? Two hundred? Whatever the nature of the inert material below me, it was hard to reconcile with the animated, disturbed, but generally vertical and breathing version of Henry that I knew. I felt like crying, but couldn't.

Yes, I thought—almost with relief—it happened.

two

Trashings

Let me explain. Let me try to explain something about myself, which in turn may explain why Henry and I were friends. Let me first say, though, that this is not easy.

When I was five years old, I talked to Jesus. And Jesus talked to me.

At the time I was going to a religious school and attended mandatory services daily. I kneeled and prayed and sang along with my classmates, but my conversation with Jesus went on all day. In the evening Jesus would ask me questions about the Christian morality of my behavior during the day (such is the collective weight of my Puritan heritage that I believed I was a sinner at five years old), and I would be compelled—some mysterious elusive rule in my mind forced this to be so—to answer him out loud. To his steady line of questioning, I would say yes or no and sometimes elaborate on the reasons for my sinning. A further rule of this conversation was that other people had to be around to hear me. So at dinnertime I would draw my face away from the table and say softly yes or no in response to a series of imaginary questions. My two older brothers, John and Tom, laughed and teased me; my parents thought it was all a little strange but just sort of shrugged it off, as they were, and are, prone to do with any odd behavior. Within a few months the phase passed—Jesus presumably moved on to interrogate somebody else—and I fully rejoined my family at the dinner table. My parents, if they even remembered these odd private conversations, no doubt sighed with relief.

But throughout my uneventful and largely happy childhood, I was periodically troubled by similar ripples of strange thoughts and compulsions:

When I was seven or eight, when I was putting together at night the clothes I was going to wear to school the next day, a voice would enter my mind. It would tell me to wear, for example, the red shirt and not the blue shirt: if I wore the blue shirt, the voice said, I would die on my twenty-first birthday. And so I would wear the red shirt.

When I was nine or ten, riding in the backseat of my parents' Ford Country Squire station wagon, I would have to count telephone poles as we sped past them. 1, 2, 3 . . . 12, 13, 14 . . . 32, 33, 34. I hated being forced to count telephone poles. It seemed deeply perverse to me, and yet I couldn't get my mind onto something else. I would sweat and get agitated and wish I didn't have to count, but the voice would continue: 110, 111, 112 . . . Eventually I would be overcome by the staggering, crippling fear that I would have to count telephone polls for the rest of my life.

When I was ten or eleven, I would feel obliged to count the number of times I breathed or blinked. I would sit in class, hating the fact that I was counting such a ludicrous thing.

When I was twelve or thirteen, sex entered the picture. Well, not sex exactly—not actual sex, I was not brave enough for that—but masturbation and ideas about sex. In particular, the whole idea of erections was deeply unsettling to me.

It's bizarre, but I became obsessed with the idea of getting an erection in a public place. I feared—no, fear is not the word, torment is—that people would observe me with an erection. This was so embarrassing, so prurient, so awful that I simply could not tolerate it. At St. Joe's I would sit in class and think, no, no, please, I can't get an erection. Please, no. The one time I did get a one, and walked down the hallways with my book covering my crotch, I wished I had died. I felt like I should be punished for my sin. While I was entering puberty and feeling excited and powerful and sexualized in a way that I never had before, I couldn't escape what seemed like an innate belief that the simple of act of getting an erection was fundamentally wrong, and worse, destructive. It all seemed overwhelmingly raw and primitive, something to recoil from and never to return. It seemed that if I got an erection in public, something bad must inevitably result from that, as in a logic equation: If p, then q. If an erection, then calamity. Exactly what that calamity was, I never knew—I just had a sense of impending doom, like something out of a medieval painting of hell. I must say, the source of my egregiously censorious nature is even now slightly mystifying to me—other than that I seem to have been particularly adept at absorbing the legacy of centuries' worth of Protestant discomfort with sexuality.

Throughout it all, despite the intermittent and horrific intensity of these thoughts, I always eventually succeeded at letting them go and slipping back to my preferred version of reality, which generally entailed getting good grades, being cheerful and well liked in an off-kilter sort of way: in short, being my own good-natured, if slightly eccentric, version of the all-American boy. (As a friend said to me in college, "You're very all-American—in a Jack Nicholson kind of way.") I became expert at shutting down the offending intrusions and getting back to work. I pretended that they had never even happened. It was in this way, I'm sure, that I perfected my ability to mentally ostracize anything, such as Henry's memory, that I did not want to think about.

All of these obsessions I kept to myself. I never even considered talking about them to my parents. My father was an imposing six-foot four-inch workaholic who didn't, I thought, have time for such crazy interruptions, and my stiff-upper-lip mother does not complain or like to hear complaints. And even though Henry and Nick accompanied me—that is, were physically present—during these tortured mental passages, I never breathed a word to them either. Private tribulations are not what teenage boys talk to each other about. Had I thought to find out, I could have learned that all my nonsensical ruminations were highly typical, indeed textbook illustrations, of the early onset of a not uncommon malady called obsessive compulsive disorder. But that could never have happened, because to seek out such information would have required that I recognize that something was wrong, which, despite the presence of these occasionally seismic and crippling internal shocks, I was entirely unwilling to do.

In retrospect, the only thing clear to me is that these brutal ripples of thought served to bring me closer to Henry. It was my own internal sense of disturbance that made me feel close to him, to want to spend time with him; without them I would have been free to dismiss Henry and his pathologies as so much absurd nonsense.

All of which is an involved way of saying that without the obsessions, there would have been no Henry; and without Henry, there would have been no black chair.

◦ ◦ ◦

Henry had that look in his eyes, that hard and wired look that I had come to associate that fall with the recent ingestion of various illicit substances, usually some carefully measured mixture of speed, LSD, and scotch. That trio of substances had been Henry's drugs of choice that fall, the fall of his freshman year at Wilson, when we were both eighteen years old—serving the purposes of stimulation, hallucination, and relaxation, respectively. Henry was also sweating from the sheer aerobic exertion of grabbing one object after another and then pelting them, as hard as he possibly could, against the cinder-block walls of his single dormitory room. Henry was, in fact, destroying everything around him. He took beer bottles, wine bottles, cans, rocks, ashtrays, coffee mugs, a pair of shoes, some socks, a clock radio, shirts, books, pens, nails, a hairbrush, and tape cassettes and hurled them one by one against the wall. The cinder block was wonderful for breaking things against. The glass and china items hit the wall with a spectacularly violent sound and exploded into hundreds of little pieces. Shards flew out the door and into the hallway. Standing near the door, I had to step back repeatedly to avoid getting hit. Henry laughed maniacally after each particularly impressive explosion. He did all this to the intensely loud musical accompaniment of the Talking Heads.

After the supply of more-accessible objects was depleted, Henry turned to his records. Henry kept a meticulous collection of perhaps a thousand albums, almost exclusively of the punk rock genre. Under more sober circumstances, he maintained them fastidiously, cleaning them after each listening and placing them back on the shelf in alphabetical order. But now he randomly grabbed the albums, removed the black vinyl discs from their inner sleeves, and threw them, Frisbee-like, against the wall. For minutes he destroyed records by bands with names like Joy Division, Killing Joke, the Dead Kennedys, Throbbing Gristle, Suicidal Tendencies, Gang of Four, the Sex Pistols, The Clash. Upon impact the discs cracked into great spiky shapes and fell to the floor.

After a while Henry got into a certain running rhythm, getting better and better at the repetitive process of grabbing and throwing, so that soon he was able to destroy an album every ten seconds or so. He didn't stop until he'd made a significant dent in his collection, and the remains of what were once sixty albums lay in pieces on the floor.

He paused for air. On our regular nocturnal walks around Cold River, Henry was forever picking up objects he found on the street —pieces of wire, wood, branches, rubber, sponges, whatever—and stuffing them in his pockets. Back in his room, he built out of the objects miniature sculptural worlds on the tops of cabinets and on windowsills. Henry now found the nests of these serene creations and hurled them, these handfuls of wire and rubber and wood, to the wall. He didn't stop until all the surfaces of the room were clean.

◦ ◦ ◦

As the destruction mounted, amazed hall-mates congregated in the corridor behind me. I turned around to see that the predominant expression on their faces was fear, Henry's performance perhaps not a scene envisioned for their freshman year. The faces of the dorm-mates looked at me beseechingly, as if I should intervene. I did nothing, of course, and after a while they returned to the still of their rooms to resume the study of organic chemistry or French literature, feeling perhaps just a little more unsettled than they had before.

But Henry stopped eventually, panting. He wasn't in good shape and could keep up the pace only for so long. For the first time he seemed to fully notice that I was there.

"What's going on, man?" I said, over the Talking Heads.

"Nothing much," he said.

"Is everything okay?" I said.

"Oh, everything is wonderful, just great," Henry said. And, indeed, he seemed genuinely happy.

He collapsed on the mattress, which was now upside down and in the corner, and drank directly from a surviving bottle of scotch.

"Want some?" he asked.

"Sure," I said, although I was unaccustomed to the harder stuff.

We sat among the wreckage, drinking and talking. After a while we went for a walk around the campus, and Henry collected more objects from the street, and then, with uncharacteristic decisiveness, we decided to walk four miles each way to the 7-11. After the unaccustomed exertion of the trashing, Henry needed M&M's. "I need chocolate," he announced, with gravity.

Halfway to the 7-11, Henry collapsed and lay down on the double yellow line in the middle of the road. He was laughing hysterically. "Get up, man!" I said. "A car could come and run you over." He didn't get up. I tried to drag him. It was hard to move him more than a few feet. He was still laughing.

"You're a funkbutt, and I'm a punkbutt!" he shouted at me.

"What?" I said.

"You're a funkbutt, and I'm a punkbutt!"

"What the hell are you talking about?" I said.

"You're a funkbutt, and I'm a punkbutt!" Henry shouted it a hundred more times.

I pretended I didn't understand, but I did. Henry was accusing me of disloyalty. Recently I had gone to see the pop star Prince in concert. It was before he became widely known, and I was just about the only white person there. Afterward I had raved to Henry about what an amazing musician Prince was. To Henry, this was nothing less than a change in religion, a rejection of the punk music that he had avidly, and I not so avidly, loved in the last few years. I was selling out. I was no longer a true believer. I was possibly no longer his friend.

That whole night of the first trashing and the pilgrimage to the 7-11 I acted as if nothing unusual had happened. But if I had thought about things for even a moment, I would have realized that Henry was destroying not only his room but also the world of his parents, who had spent their entire careers teaching in the English Department of the college. In fact, his parents' home was only about three hundred yards from Henry's dorm, on the edge of the campus.

The trashings became a regular occurrence that fall, a ritual and almost choreographed event. Gradually, inexorably, the supplies of breakable objects would build up again. An impressive collection of wine and beer bottles would suddenly appear, just waiting to be tossed. Henry and I would be walking along at night, and he'd mutter, almost to himself, "I feel a trashing coming on," or "I think it's time."

In the mornings after a trashing (or afternoons actually, as he never got up until one or two), Henry meticulously cleaned up the ruins.

I would return the next day to find his room pristine and intact, if quite a bit more barren than before. The only evidence of the violence would be tiny shards of glass, like salt, that he would miss sweeping up, usually to be found under the bed or in the corners. If you put the sole of your shoe on them they would squeak, like chalk on a blackboard.

Henry's other contribution to campus life that fall was as a graffiti artist. In the time between trashings and taking drugs, he entered every bathroom on campus and drew this on the walls:

Henry spent so much time drawing this strange cartoon that for a distinct period in that fall of 1980 you could barely go anywhere on campus without spotting Boontan. "I know who created that," I would think with a strange feeling of pride. I never knew what the symbol meant. But I did, of course: Boontan meant nothing, and that's exactly why Henry spent hours drawing it everywhere he could.

When I left that night after the first trashing, some freshmen women, recognizing me as Henry's friend, afforded me a wide berth in the hallway, as if I might spontaneously attack them. There was something about their fear, and my newfound notoriety as an associate of Henry's, that pleased me very much. I realize now that there was a deeply hidden part of me that admired the trashings. I felt the same rage, a rage that emanated from the peculiar obsessions that kept on passing through me, but only Henry had the courage to show it.

If it ever occurred to me (or to Nick, who as Henry's classmate at Wilson witnessed many of the same scenes) to intervene, we quickly dispelled the notion. Nick was getting more and more immersed in his course work, doing exceptionally well in school, and found the trashings a bizarre distraction. But it was more than that: we both knew that any type of earnest and direct encounter about Henry's behavior would have been way too awkward. Henry and Nick and I had been around each other for years; we had endured any number of "developmental milestones" together—homeroom elections, unending school bus rides, algebra tests, spitballs, puberty—all of which made us singularly comfortable with silent coexistence. There was no need to discuss, to share.

Besides, I was largely unmoved by Henry's displays. I often found him to be annoying, unstable, and bizarre, and at numerous points in our association considered ditching him as a friend. The previous spring I had graduated from prep school with high honors, with awards in English and math, varsity letters in track and cross-country, and a letter of acceptance to Harvard. In my headier moments, I thought that I had the potential to do something great and substantial someday, and I felt that Henry simply didn't. I felt, in essence, superior to Henry. Despite my deeply buried knowledge that I was susceptible to the regular intrusion of disturbing and crippling thoughts and compulsions, I felt that I was better than he was, and stronger. I felt so superior to him that half the time I didn't want to be around him; he was a stain, albeit an interesting one, on my pure canvas. Or that's what I made myself think.

Our roles had long since been set—I was stable (or so the world thought), he was unstable; I was successful, he was erratic; I didn't take drugs, he did; I got rewarded, he got in trouble. Henry and I had known each other since we were six. Our first meeting, I believe, was at Saturday youth athletic programs on the campus. In any contest I, being decent at sports, would be picked first or second, and then I would lobby for Henry to be selected respectably in the middle of the pack rather than where he was otherwise destined, with the fat kids at the end. (Henry wasn't fat but oddly abstracted even then, showing no interest in the kicking and throwing of balls.) In school, Henry and I were invariably at the top of the class, but we got there from different directions. I ingratiated myself with teachers and generally did the prescribed work; Henry was silent and passive, didn't appear to study, and yet got perfect scores on the tests.

I think the great divide between Henry and me, or should I say between Henry and his own lucidity, began with the infusion of great quantities of LSD into his body. Before LSD, Henry was weird, aloof, abstracted, troubled, and probably deeply unhappy, but he was not disordered. After LSD, the pieces never fit back together again. His mind remained powerful (it may even have become more powerful), but he appeared to lose his ability to make distinctions, to consider things separately and either accept or reject them. He seemed to have lost the ability to do things in any planned or measured fashion. In place of clarity, a sort of permanent silliness set in.

In March of our junior year, when I was on vacation from Andover, Henry and I had lunch in a pizza parlor in Cold River. I hadn't seen him for a little while, and I noticed he had changed. He looked unhealthier, had developed acne, and had thickened somehow. There was a hardness in his eyes that seemed to me to be both ethereal and resolute.

"I've experienced a revelation," he said.

"What is it?"

"LSD . . . Once you've taken it, Charlie, you'll never be the same. You will never see things in the same way."

I could tell he wasn't the same. I was horrified. A few years later I discovered the joys of alcohol, often in Henry's company, but substances like LSD scared me.

I have asked a number of psychiatrists whether LSD can induce long-term psychosis, even after the drug itself has left the system. I have received contradictory responses, but in most instances the answer has been no. Based on my experience, I would doubt that. Another faculty child, whom Henry and I both knew, was rumored to have taken a hundred tabs of LSD in a single day, while a junior at Exeter.

Five years later this once rather timid, preppy boy, considered at one time to be a prodigy in mathematics, became permanently psychotic, unable to work even at menial jobs and given to robbing his parents for drug money. The last time I saw him he spoke to me earnestly and quite psychotically about Jesus Christ and handguns.

In the autumn of the trashings, I would get up at six thirty to go to my job at an orchard in the countryside near Cold River. I had decided to take a year off before going to Harvard. In the first part of the year I was going to work at the orchard, and in the second I was going to live with my parents, who would be on sabbatical in Rome, and then travel around Europe. It would be, I thought self-consciously, my version of the Grand Tour that people like Henry Adams and Henry James made in the previous century.

In the early part of the fall I picked apples with a crew of Jamaican migrant workers. My productivity was about half of theirs, 130 bushels in a day to their 250. When the apple season slowed, I was transferred to the cider mill. We poured the crates of apples onto a conveyor belt, where they were hacked into pumice by a buzzing cylinder lined with thick razorlike blades. The collision of the apples with the blades produced a white noise—you couldn't hear people speak above it even if they shouted—that we lived in for eight hours a day.

I'm sure I was the only employee at the orchard who read Thoreau on his lunch break. Or tried to read Thoreau. I found him boring and could never read more than a few pages at a time. But I was taken by the idea that I was immersing myself in a kind of rural New England purity, that after excelling academically in high school, I would, for a while at least, be part of the land.

I probably mumbled something to Henry about my trip to Europe, probably just a few days before I left. We were eighteen, and there were no grand pronouncements of our comings and goings and reunions, just a simultaneous existence during the times we happened to be together. Besides, I kept from Henry my grander schemes. My trip to Europe I considered a rounding out of my education, the accumulation of an additional veneer of sophistication on my character. I knew that Henry would not be particularly interested in or impressed by any of it. Henry never had much regard for self-improvement or what might look appealing on his résumé. I don't think I ever actually said good-bye to him before I left.

A few weeks later I found myself, surreally, in a palatial, marble-floored apartment in Rome. The exchange rate of the Italian lira to the dollar was favorable, allowing my father to rent a place we could never have afforded in America. Our elaborate apartment had about eight rooms, two balconies, and overlooked a piazza. There was a library, filled with Italian- and English-language novels. For the first time I felt that my family was rich. And I had absolutely nothing that I had to do. It was all a rather bizarre contrast from my recent history of pressing cider in New England. I enrolled in Italian classes but spent most days lazily hanging out in cafés, touring the hills and monuments of the city, and more than anything, reading. As my Italian got better, I fantasized about meeting lovely Italian girls, but I never did. I must have read everything by Hemingway, Fitzgerald, J. D. Salinger, and Graham Greene during those months. But after three months of it, I was bored and prematurely world-weary. I was more prone than before to the ugly intrusive thoughts about repeating words and strange sexual stuff. To my surprise, I missed Nick and Henry.

In April I traveled north, first to the French Riviera and Antibes, then Paris, then London, staying with friends and distant relatives along the way. I spent most of my days alone, walking the streets of the great capitals of Europe, reading, and going to cafés and museums, always in my now-typical state of abstraction. The most satisfying part of the trip was a week I spent fishing and hiking on the Isle of Harris, in Outer Hebrides of Scotland. The Hebrides themselves were a revelation, unlike anywhere else I'd ever been. Unspoiled, nearly empty and treeless, the islands felt otherworldly. I wondered if I was on the moon. Beaches of white sand stretched for miles, and there was absolutely nobody around. There were miles and miles of heather and gorse and the occasional scrubby bush. The temperature of the ocean, in May, was not much above freezing. I fished in the lochs and walked all day on the violently precipitous hills of the island. There was something about the tripartite purity of the elements in the Hebrides—equal parts water, air, and earth—that dissipated my ennui. I remember lying on the desolate Hebridean sands reading *The*

Great Gatsby, soaking up the one or two hours of precious afternoon sun, and feeling truly happy for the first time since I left Cold River. Toward the conclusion of my Grand Tour of Europe, I read a short story called "The Christian Roommates," by John Updike. The story is about a young man's freshman year at Harvard. Orson is from South Dakota and arrives at the university with high expectations. He is ambitious and competitive but rather unimaginative, the son of a doctor who wanted to be a doctor—one of those people who have their entire life planned out by age twelve. His roommate, named Hub, is a pacifist vegetarian wrestler from Oregon. Hub is abstemious but rather self-righteous in his beliefs, which include defying his state's draft board in objection to the Korean War. The two roommates grate on each other, but benignly so. Orson grows to hate Hub's unorthodoxies; Hub, however, professes nothing but love for Orson. In the midst of the dour Massachusetts winter, Hub proudly returns to the dormitory with a parking meter that has become dislodged after being struck by a car. Hub regards the meter as properly belonging to the people and plans to donate its contents to charity. Orson, enraged at Hub's disregard for convention, let alone the law, tries to pry the parking meter away from him. In the tussle, Orson wrestles Hub to the ground and tries to strangle him. Hub, the wrestler, is able to deflect any serious blows, and no real damage is done. The two roommates even make up in their way. Orson goes on to medical school, becomes a doctor, marries his high school sweetheart, and moves back to South Dakota. Everything has gone according to plan, but something—some deep spiritual thing—in Orson has been permanently altered, or removed. I read the story with a sort of painful interest. I found it compelling but rather preposterous. I was absolutely certain that my experience at Harvard would be nothing like that.

In June I flew from Paris to Boston and took a bus across New England to Cold River. I was relieved to be home. It was June, and after the spring rains the land in New England seemed an endlessly rolling, rich green lawn. American flags adorned vinyl-sided houses, men mowed their lawns, people drove around in huge cars past convenience stores and malls. Compared to Italy, America seemed clumsy and young. I arrived in darkness at my parents' empty home in Cold River. The next morning the first thing I did was call Nick to catch up.

"What's happening, man?" I said.

"Nothing much," Nick said.

Nick told me that his freshman year had ended well. He had gotten straight As and was working for the Wilson physical plant department for the summer, washing security cars.

"It's the easiest job I've ever had. Our required quota is to wash exactly two cars a day," he said. "But we have to wash them really well," he added.

Nick said that in the frequent downtime he explained the philosophies of Camus to the college's maintenance workers.

"And do they like Camus?" I said.

"Well, put it this way, I'm still trying to get them not to pronounce it Came-us," Nick said. "But other than that, they're very intrigued," he laughed.

"Do they hate you yet?" I said.

"Hell no, I'm one of the guys!" Nick laughed, indignant.

"And how's Henry?" I asked.

"Henry," he paused. "You don't know? Oh . . . well, Henry tried to kill himself . . . Jeez, I thought you knew. It must have been shortly after you left . . . He got kicked out of the university, because of the trashings, and he took an overdose of pills in the bathroom of his parents' house. His father found him, and they pumped his stomach at the hospital."

I felt a rush of acid to my stomach.

"Is he okay?"

"Well, physically, yeah. He didn't do any real damage, if that's what you're asking, because his father found him in time. I guess it was some pills that he'd been saving up. They transferred him to the psychiatric unit of the hospital. He was there for a while. He's home now. I guess he's okay . . . playing a fucking guitar all day long. He won't talk to me about anything that happened . . ." As Nick spoke, I found myself for some reason focusing very deeply on the chair I was sitting in. I remember that it was a gray angular armchair made out of acrylic fabric with thin diagonal white stripes. I heard every word Nick said, and understood, I think, its implications, but I also found as he spoke that I lost myself in the microcosm of the chair and its individual strands of fabric.

"Oh yeah, the Courts moved," Nick said. "They sold the house after it happened, and they're living in a condo now, a few miles from town." With a nervous hand I wrote down the address.

After I hung up the phone I looked at myself in the glass sliding door that led out of the basement. In the reflection of the door, I saw I was profusely sweating, my shirt soaked through. There was a raw feeling deep in my stomach. I thought, "It's all different now. Henry wanted to die."

Consistent with my desire to avoid things, I went immediately to bed. But it wasn't that easy. Henry wanted to die . . . He wanted to die . . . He could have died . . . He wanted to die . . . Those words rebounded through my brain as I tried to sleep that night.

⊸ ⊸ ⊸

The Courts' new home was in a brand-new development, on a piece of land that I distantly remembered had been a farm. The complex was clean and geometrical, a boxlike maze of dwellings, all with fresh pine shingles and newly mown lawns.

I stood at the front door of the Courts' new home, considering whether to ring the doorbell. The morning was cloudless and blue, one of those rare New England summer days with no humidity, and I thought that I didn't really have to see Henry again; I could just walk out into the clear blue day and leave him and his problems behind forever. I feared seeing him. I was worried that I would be somehow infected with Henry's despair—it would be like a virus that would work its way into me. As I write now, at my desk at the New York City shelter, I can see myself clearly, very clearly, on that doorstep—a tall, thin, well-meaning, awkward eighteen-year-old, neither man nor boy. I see myself teetering—deciding whether to ring the doorbell or to escape, to walk away from Henry and his difficulties forever and out into that unblemished blue day.

But just then, Mrs. Court, Henry's mother, came to the door.

"Oh, Charlie, you're back! Henry will be so thrilled to see you!" she said. "Come in!" she all but implored. She looked like Henry, although shorter and wider. She had the same strong features, the same obvious intelligence. And both of them dyed their hair the same lurid orange hue.

"Come in! How was your trip? Are your parents home yet?" Even for her, she was unusually solicitous. But I felt she was less glad to see me than the idea of me, hoping that I would bestow on Henry a stability he otherwise lacked.

Henry, I knew, hated her. He never stated his reasons, but I could pretty much figure them out. She was high-strung, often seeming to be on the verge of some unknown hysteria. Lacking a sense of discretion, she overwhelmed people, not appearing to have a firm grasp psychologically on where she ended and you began. While she was typically spirited and energetic, those qualities could turn quickly into being intrusive and dominating.

I remember, after Henry died, she telephoned my house, drunk, and asked for my mother. She was slurring her words. "Tell your mother that my colleague in the English department"—she said his name—"is suffering from a serious depression but is refusing all help. I've been doing everything I can. See if your mother can get him to go to a doctor."

"I'll give her the message," I said, and didn't.

In high school, when Henry and I ran track together, Mrs. Court sometimes drove us home. She took over the conversation with annoying questions about our day and made allusions to the British literature that she was steeped in, and that we, as fourteen-year-olds, cared nothing about. She would talk on and on about Ford Madox Ford (whose masterwork *The Good Soldier*, I recently read and was not all surprised to learn that two of its principal characters commit suicide.) Or she would talk about the stock market. For all her literary interests, she was apparently quite effective at managing the not insignificant amount of money she had inherited from her industrialist father. I would do my best to be polite and summon an interest in Virginia Woolf, Evelyn Waugh, the War Poets, all of which of course had no meaning for me. Henry stared angrily, silently out the window as his mother nattered on.

Mrs. Court led me noisily down the newly painted hall to see Henry.

"Charlie is here, Henry!" Mrs. Court said, as we reached the door to his room.

Silence from inside the room.

I knocked. More silence. Mrs. Court having departed, I opened the door and found Henry lying, perfectly alert, on a futon on the floor.

"What's up, man?" I said.

"Nothing much," he said.

Henry lay below me, defeated-looking. His head was shorn, and he was thinner. It seemed that his face was more creased looking, and his spirit less voluble. His hair was still dyed orange, but less emphatically so than in the fall. It was as if a kind of purging had occurred. I looked around to find an immaculately clean room; Henry seemed to have surrounded himself with minimalism. There were few objects, and therefore little to destroy. In the large space there was only the futon, a stereo and record collection (much sparser than it had been in the fall), and two new additions: an electric bass guitar with an amplifier and, oddly, a motorcycle. By the bed were books by Carlos Castaneda and Herman Hesse. I wondered if they signaled a newly found existential orientation.

I tried again. "So how are you, man?" I said.

"Fine," he said, absurdly.

I kept on thinking that despite Nick's telling me that Henry had overdosed on pills, he must instead have slashed his wrists with a razor blade. Isn't that how people first try to kill themselves, before they find better, more-subtle methods? I furtively scanned his wrists for scars. I now know that Henry was brought first to the emergency room, had his stomach pumped, was transferred to the psychiatric unit of the hospital in a nearby city, then transferred again to a "residential treatment center" in upstate New York. Nick told me recently about visiting Henry in the hospital. Nick actually asked him why he wanted to kill himself. Henry replied only, "I wanted to die," and left it at that. At some point Nick said, "I love you, you know," to which Henry responded, "Yeah, I know." Henry quickly diverted the conversation to the guards and orderlies, who, he said, would slap you around if you acted up. Apparently he spoke from experience. Henry said they were like the thought-control goons in Pink Floyd's *The Wall*, which was his favorite album at the time.

But it was not for me to delve into that territory. I realize now that this was the first of two moments at which Henry and I could have changed the essentially superficial tenor of our relationship. But we both let it pass that afternoon.

It never occurred to me to ask:

"Why did you want to kill yourself?"

or

"What was going on?"

or

"Why did you trash your room?"

or

"What exactly was so painful?"

Instead, I spoke of the beaches in the Hebrides, the varieties and robustness of British beer, about how punk had become so omnipresent in London that even bank tellers had green hair and clothespins hanging from their ears. Henry laughed.

And so we talked about nothing. We talked about albums that had come out in the months since I left. I distinctly recall that we talked at length about Elvis Costello. Henry pulled out a couple of new records and played me a couple of tunes on his stereo. We listened, in silence, to the music.

I spotted, nearly hidden in the corner, a series of drawings. There were hundreds of sketches, in pencil, pen and ink, watercolor. All were renderings of the same image—a series of parallel lines of varying widths with a code of numbers at the bottom. They looked cold and very technological.

"What are these?" I asked.

"Oh that . . . um . . . that's the Universal Price Code," Henry said, rather timidly.

"What's that?"

"You mean you haven't heard of the UPC code? They put it on all products now . . . if you go to the supermarket, most cans and food products have it stamped on them somewhere. They scan them through the lasers at the checkout counter and it automatically registers the price."

Apparently this new technology had proliferated while I was away.

"And why exactly are you drawing them?" I asked.

"Uh . . ." Henry said. "Well, you know how the painters in the Renaissance painted the crucifixion over and over again?"

"Yes," I said.

"Well, I think if they were living now, I bet they'd be painting the UPC code. It's like the symbol of our times—or will be—just the way Christ was back then."

I couldn't decide whether Henry was being crazy or brilliant, or both. I do know that the UPC code has more daily prominence in our lives than images of Christ, or just about any other symbol. I wish I had some of those drawings now.

"That's cool," I said.

I looked at the gleaming motorcycle.

"It's brand new," Henry said, relieved, I think, that I was paying attention to something else. "It makes for easy escapes," he said, with his old mischievous grin. "You could start it in the room, drive it across the neatly tended condo lawn, and immediately get out on the road . . ."

At which point Henry rose from the futon, put on his shoes, opened the screen door that led out to a slate patio, got onto the motorcycle, started the engine, gestured for me to get on, and drove out of the room. Within seconds we were driving sixty miles an hour through the deep green fast-flowing countryside of Cold River.

◆ ◆ ◆

That summer I washed and Henry dried.

It surprised me how well Henry washed and dried dishes. I figured that having taken so many drugs and being a generally abstracted and intellectual sort of person he would have been unable to focus for hours and hours on dirty plates. I would have thought his brain was permanently addled by clouds of marijuana. But he excelled at dishwashing.

Since it wasn't cider season when I returned to Cold River, I applied for a position as a dishwasher at the busiest restaurant in town. On a night when the usual dishwasher got drunk and didn't show up, I was called at home. An hour later I found myself elbow deep in a sink filled with dishes, grease, and near-toxic industrial-strength detergent. After I established my dishwashing expertise, I, without much confidence, recommended Henry for the job as well. Soon we found ourselves side-by-side in grease.

As dishwashers, Henry and I were treated like trash. We loved it. We dressed the part. I grew my hair long and stringy, while Henry turned more abrasively punk. We wore work boots and jeans and leather, and acted as if we'd been shaken out of the trees from the rural communities around Cold River. There was a curious relief from the pressure of achievement. In the murk of dishwater, we could drop our shared family burdens of academic purity and righteousness. It had always been assumed that Henry and I, good at school when we chose to be, would follow our parents in some fashion. If we weren't going to be scholars exactly, then it was expected that we be something . . . noble.

Dishwashing was a nice antithesis to nobility. For once we were under no pressure except to wash three hundred sets of dishes a night. But while I was happy washing dishes, for me it was merely the donning of an image that pleased me at the time. I knew I wouldn't be washing dishes for long. For Henry, though, it seemed more than a flirtation. I felt that he reveled in the role a bit too much. He began hanging out with the janitor, whom I disliked, a mean, demented-looking pothead. Henry started getting high with him on his breaks. He would return to my side red-eyed and ethereal and not working with his former energy. I resented this and remained silent, until he cracked some joke and made me laugh.

Toward the end of the summer I was promoted to busboy, a serious promotion in the restaurant world, like going from private to sergeant. I suddenly mattered in the hierarchy of the restaurant. (The intense hierarchy of restaurants, all restaurants, is something that people who have never worked in them cannot possibly understand.) When I left for college, Henry took my place. Being a busboy would be the apex of his career.

⋅❖ ⋅❖ ⋅❖

In August of our summer of dishwashing, Henry called me one morning, very early. We never got up early.

"Wanna go for a trip?" he asked.

I didn't know what to say. Henry never initiated things.

Within fifteen minutes, he came up our driveway in his mother's blue Volvo. For reasons he never explained, he wanted to show me a particular town on the coast. A couple of hours later, we were there.

Beach Hill is an old Victorian town, set on a long isthmus that travels out into the Atlantic. While its homes still sell for millions, it's a town that has seen better days. There was a touch of old-money decay to the place: many of the old mansions needed painting and seemed sporadically occupied; the carousel was no longer used. There was one main block with an ice cream parlor and boutiques. We ate ice cream for breakfast. Henry's hair caused the other diners mild concern as we sat in the ice cream parlor, which was decorated all in pink. Henry, again with uncharacteristic vigor, stated that he wanted to show me the isthmus. We hopped a fence and walked out toward the ocean for what seemed like a mile on an increasingly narrow strip of land. The air was fresh and cold. At the very end we came on some half-completed brick structures that looked as if they had once had a defensive purpose, like ramparts.

"In World War I, the Americans feared the Germans would attack New York City by coming around this side of Long Island, through the Sound," Henry explained. "These are the remains of the ramparts built to prevent that. There used to be cannons here." Henry seemed pleased by this notion. If I had analyzed it then, which I surely didn't, I would have realized that it made every sense that Henry was drawn to this barren place. For one thing, he could not have found a more remote spot on the entire East Coast of America. And the unrealized potential of the ramparts—the fact that they were never used; that they were, in fact, powerful yet impotent—mimicked Henry's feckless nature perfectly.

We lay in the grass by the ramparts for a long while, at least an hour or two, and then we walked back. We ate more ice cream in the pink parlor for lunch, and then walked through the maze of craggy old mansions on the hillsides overlooking the water. I understood why it all appealed to Henry—there was a touch of the gothic to it. It seemed like odd things happened and old families lived in those mansions . . . dusty hallways, rotting food, stacks of unpaid bills, decay, incest . . . at least I think that's probably what Henry liked to think.

On the way home we took the back roads, past farms on straight roads lined with telephone poles. We drove home in silence. The patter and joking and trashings had stopped. There had been no need to speak. I was home, and I was at home with him. For once we were comfortable in our own skins. I was at peace. Maybe I'm wrong, but I believe on that day, anyway, Henry felt the exultancy of the ex-suicide, the happiness of his (briefly, as it turned out) extended existence in the world.

After he dropped me off at home, I looked at my sunburned face in the mirror. It had been a most excellent day spent looking at waves.

three

The Right Anguishes

According to my grandmother's handwritten notes, which I came across after her death, two Barber brothers sailed from County Tyrone, northern Ireland, for the New World in 1713. The ship was wrecked in a storm a few miles off the coast of Massachusetts. The two brothers, William and Joseph, were the only two persons to swim ashore. All the other passengers perished in the frigid waters of the North Atlantic.

I like to think of this story (apocryphal or not, my grandmother, a sober-minded woman, a farmer's wife, a scholar manqué, would not have been the one to fabricate it) as the first indicator of a particular family talent for endurance—a sheer obstinate ability to keep on doing something under poor conditions. Collectively my family seems to share a capacity for repetition. Typically there is nothing particularly brilliant or striking about what any of us have done, whether it be farming or pressing cider or investment banking, but as a group we seem to have the ability to pursue something to the end. Whether I share this ability has been a matter of continual speculation among my elders.

From time to time, in darker moments, I like to summon the image of William and Joseph breaking through the waves. Thinking of them soothes me. When I think of the last weekend that Nick and I spent with Henry, and the oblivion that was shortly to follow, I like to balance out the horror of that experience with the vision of William and Joseph struggling to reach the shores of Massachusetts. I see them pushing through the fatal waters of the North Atlantic, glimpsing brief images of the New World between waves, moving ever so slowly toward the shore. They must have thought they were going to die. I see one brother pulling the other through the water. I can hear them sputtering for air, perhaps removing their clothes to stay afloat. I see them, probably not too many moments from death, pushing up onto the rocky shore. Probably they huddled together for hours for warmth, then looked in vain for other survivors. Who knows where they looked for shelter, or where they went, how far the nearest town was. Maybe they had to fight off Indians or other settlers. At times they must have wished they had died with everybody else. Eventually Joseph, my great-great-great-great-great-great-grandfather, after years of effort, established a farm in Weston, Massachusetts, not forty miles from where he washed ashore. Yes, I like to think of William and Joseph. To me they balance out Henry's choice, in a farmhouse not unlike the one Joseph built, and only a hundred miles away.

⋄⋄ ⋄⋄ ⋄⋄

On another October night, two years after Henry's season of trashings and my cider mill autumn, I was impatient. It was Friday night and I wanted to leave. I sat by the window in the darkness of the hall of my parents' house, awaiting the slow movement of the headlights of Nick's car climbing the driveway. I wanted Nick to take me away, from Cold River, myself, and my morbid fantasies.

With relief, I heard the familiar rattle of his old Ford Maverick.

"Ready to go?" Nick said at the front door.

"Yes, but my mother wants to say hello."

"Nick!" She appeared, greeting him warmly. "Would you like some tea?" she said in her soft way. My mother is originally from England, and now speaks in a Katherine Hepburn–like hybrid English-American accent.

My mother always liked Nick. She liked Nick as much as she disliked Henry, whom she regarded as passive and feckless. She liked to talk to Nick about the courses he took at Wilson, courses in which he never received anything less than an A minus—unlike her son, who had recently and quite inexplicably dropped out of Harvard. Nick appeared to her, under the circumstances, as less enigmatic. He was almost macho, with thick curly hair, a broad face, a moustache, and dark Sicilian skin. He spoke with a working-class New England accent, had the wide body of a nose tackle, and dressed like a slightly bohemian shoe salesman. And yet Nick could speak freely and knowledgeably about philosophy and literature, could quote Sartre, Camus, and Kierkegaard at will. Particularly Camus, of course—he could quote lines from *The Stranger* and *The Fall* and *The Myth of Sisyphus* verbatim. Nick spoke with expertise about these writers in a thoroughly unpretentious manner. He could switch in a second from talking about Camus' conflict with Sartre to the status of the New York Giants backfield. As opposed to how she felt about Nick, my mother was mystified by her son, he of the apparent promise and privilege, who had a year ago withdrawn from college on short notice, returned to Cold River, and—of all things!—returned to his former job as a busboy. In numerous ways and at numerous times, she and her husband had requested explanations of his behavior, but received none. That, of course, was the last thing I was going to do—tell my parents about what had really happened at Harvard.

My mother poured the tea. I sat quietly at the table, considering the upcoming weekend with Henry. Nick and I hadn't seen him since he'd disappeared six months before. At the time of his disappearance, Henry and I had been living in a forlorn little house on the edge of campus, where we lived a strange and marginal existence together. We lived with four Wilson students, one of whom, I read in the alumni magazine, died of AIDS a few years ago. Henry and I, both newly minted college dropouts, had returned to the restaurant and taken back our jobs as busboys. I worked the day shift, Henry the night shift; as a result, we saw little of each other, but we lived parallel lives of manual labor amid the disapproval of our families. Henry appeared to be more than usually remote and forlorn and unknowable during the time we lived in that house—or perhaps, because I was near him all the time, I simply noticed it more. He also seemed to be particularly pale and dissolute-looking—using drugs of all kinds, I'm sure, but always away from me. It was during this period that he got into an accident on his motorcycle and was thrown onto the road, breaking his jaw. His jaw was wired shut for a few weeks, preventing him from speaking, although he spoke so little that it didn't seem to matter much. He ate applesauce and yogurt for a month. In the late afternoons, after his shift and before mine, we would sometimes drink beer and listen to records; occasionally we would drive to local diners and eat bad food.

I would drink coffee while Henry smoked Camels. But I recall all those times like dark, silent movies, in which we never actually spoke.

So it was in keeping with this that Henry never told me of his imminent travel plans; as far as I was concerned, he simply disappeared one day, along with his blue van. But John, another friend of all of ours, happened to be present when Henry drove away one afternoon. John said that right before Henry left he placed, with his typical sense of absurd ceremony, a paperback book on the dashboard. It was called *Microbe Hunters*, and featured on its cover a drawing of a square-looking scientist peering through a microscope. It smacked of 1950s optimism, faith in science and the ability of the rational mind to make sense of the world. I guess it was supposed to serve as a kind of bizarre talisman for the trip. So, Henry had gone away in search of microbes.

And then Henry had called me out of nowhere two weeks ago, saying that he had resurfaced at his father's farm, the family's weekend and vacation place in the Berkshires. I wasn't even aware that the Courts had such a place. No matter: Would Nick and I come visit him soon? How about a weekend near the end of the October? That would be good, we decided, it would be near the height of the foliage season. I called Nick and we set up the weekend.

At the table, Nick and my mother spoke happily as if I wasn't there: "And your courses . . . ?"

"Oh, fine . . . midterms soon . . . five books to read . . ."

" . . . and you?"

I focused on the taste of the ginger cookies. My mother always had the best, real ginger, direct from England. I heard, yet tried not to hear, the conversation.

" . . . and your parents?"

"Cool weather, this fall . . . early frost . . ."

"Oh, busy . . . volunteering at the hospital . . ."

"Well, we better get going," I said abruptly, standing up.

I picked up my bag packed with clothes for the weekend. My mother walked us to the door.

"Great to see you, Nick. Good luck with the courses."

"Thank you, Mrs. Barber."

I realized, on my way out the door, that my mother had not once mentioned our upcoming weekend with Henry.

Nick and I drove through the streets of Cold River. Even in the dark, Nick and I knew every inch of our town. We drove past the distinguished brownstone buildings of the Wilson campus, site of Nick's successes and Henry's failures, which was on the large hill at the top of the town. The college was at the top of Cold River, literally and figuratively. On our descent to the Main Street we drove past the Italian Public Market, Danny's Irish Bar and other dingy establishments, the brick Catholic churches (one for the Poles, one for the Irish, and one for the Sicilians), the all-too-numerous "Store for Rent" signs, the all-night gas stations, the brick tenements on the bad side of town, with kids loitering outside them. We then drove out of the town into what would have been called suburbia if Cold River were big enough to support suburbs. We drove past one vinyl-sided ranch house after another, all of them seemingly beige-colored, each with more or less identical mid-size American cars in their driveways. The leaves had been falling for only a few weeks now, but the lawns were neatly raked. The residents of Cold River, with few exceptions, had started the great fall ritual of creating huge piles of leaves at the side of the road. It wasn't long before Halloween, and many of the more-prosperous houses were decorated with pumpkins and orange lights and dying chrysanthemums and ghosts made of white sheets on their porches. This was our town, a marginal, forgettable town that was the entire world to us. Nick and I, and to a lesser degree Henry, thought we were unique in that we knew all the sociologies of Cold River: we knew all the professors and professionals, and having gone to the public schools and St. Joe's, and having done paper routes and worked in orchards and restaurants and so on, we knew almost everybody else. We knew the car dealers and mechanics and cops and shopkeepers. We were certain who was an alcoholic and who wasn't; we knew who was sleeping with whom; we even knew when the crazy people who hung out on the street in the bad end of town weren't taking their medication. We knew too much. Once safely out of town, we pulled onto the highway that ran for miles along the river. Nick and I talked about my mother for a while and our trepidation regarding the upcoming weekend, then turned on the radio and listened to Led Zeppelin and the Rolling Stones in silence.

I looked out on the river—silent and black and wide—and tried, at all costs, not to think about myself.

I knew enough to know that thinking about myself was absolutely the worst thing I could do. It made my blood pressure go up; it made me tense my jaw and make fists with both hands. My body would ache; I would feel whipped. It made me want to tell Nick to stop the car so I could go for a swim in the river. It was intolerable. I would be okay if I just made occasional nice conversation and listened as raptly as possible (trying not to think of anything else) to the interplay of the drums and the guitar of the Rolling Stones song on the radio.

All of this was true because in my mind at least, two years after the trashings, I had—horrors!—inexorably and completely and fully become Henry.

᯾ ᯾ ᯾

Things change. Tables turn. Winners become losers.

Things changed.

How to say this?

Shall we start with the weather? Yes, the weather . . .

It didn't snow much in Cambridge during the winter of my freshman year, and by March the exposed grass in Harvard Yard had turned a sickly yellowish color from its prolonged exposure to the cold. It had turned a gray mustardy color, an awful color. It was like the grass had become nauseous. In the few times that I actually went to class, I felt that the color of the mustard grass exactly matched my internal state.

There was a massive construction project in Harvard Square that year—the Transit Authority was building a new subway station—and the project seemed to be unique in the history of the construction business in that the work went on twenty-four hours a day. All night, on top of the bunk bed I shared with a roommate I had little to say to, I listened to the roar of heavy construction vehicles moving earth and concrete outside my bedroom window. Particularly disturbing were the high-pitched beeping sounds that the trucks and bulldozers emitted when they went in reverse. Uncomfortable, feeling clammy and sweaty from my naked plastic mattress (naked because I never used the sheets), I listened for hours to those high-pitched sounds, thinking about . . . probably nothing at all. I'd stay up until three or four, and in the beginning of the fall, I would still get up to go to calculus class at eight thirty in the morning (why I decided to study calculus I don't know, other than that I'd been told in high school that I was good at it), but after I started staying up until four or five or six or seven in the morning, I of course stopped going to class. I remember the final exam—it was fifteen pages long, and I was able to write something intelligible, actually put pencil to paper, on only six of those fifteen pages. In the definition of intellectual torture, the night before the exam I went to the all-night study hall in the cafeteria and tried to learn a semester of advanced calculus in six hours. It didn't work. But neither the construction nor calculus was really the problem.

Sometime during that fall semester I came to believe, really firmly believe, that everything I had accomplished was entirely false. There wasn't any precise moment of revelation, of course, but—maybe it was because I was really away from home for the first time—I came to see that all I had really done was just keep up. My father had gone to Harvard and Oxford, my mother to Oxford, and my two older brothers to Harvard and Yale. Being a good student and a willing son, I had merely subsumed the expectations of others and expertly fulfilled them—a difficult enough task, perhaps, but completely unoriginal. I had done what I was told. I came to feel (and I still believe this) that the whole weight of my heritage would dictate that, on say, November 13, 1982, I would be walking through Harvard Yard on my way to a calculus class thinking about . . . T. S. Eliot and sex. It hit me, with a great suffocating sense of horror, that I had been only a vessel channeling the desires of others, a mechanism, a clockwork, a clockwork orange. I had been programmed. The experiment had been a success.

This was not at all like before, when I experienced those momentary disturbances of childhood and adolescence, those doubts and fears and compulsions about what shirt to wear, about counting telephone poles, about a mortifying fear of getting erections. As deeply unpleasant, and even occasionally brutal, as those were, I was always able to get back on track and pretend that they had never happened. I was always able to resume normal relations with myself.

That fall at Harvard, the dam broke. Compulsions and obsessions of all varieties flooded into my brain, and for the first time I seemed unable to push them back. I remember stumbling numbly, painfully, through stark Harvard Yard, looking up at the silhouettes of the naked trees as they swayed eerily in the wind against the white sky. By winter, even when I did go to class, I couldn't focus on the lecturer because I was counting the number of times I blinked or breathed, or the counting the times the professor said "obvious," or counting from one to ten over and over and over again. I lost, in other words, the organicity with which one thinks, the natural and sometimes creative flow that makes up anyone's daily inner monologue. That inner conversation, that stream of consciousness that had once flowed through me easily and often richly from topic to topic, idea to idea, suddenly stopped. It froze. It froze into a single word or series of numbers. I couldn't stop myself from repeating words and numbers to myself. "Black" was a word I repeated to myself . . . black black black black black black black black black black black black black black black

I looked in the mirror and saw that I had aged. I looked pale. I lost hair. Every morning when I awoke there were hundreds of blond hairs on the pillow.

Where had my normal self gone? Why could I no longer think? Why had I become so weird?

Sometimes I could hear the lecturer's voice through the wall of black, and at other times I couldn't. This was my idea of hell—as in Dante's definition, an endless conversation with oneself—but in this case, it was a conversation that never changed.

One of the hallmarks of obsessive compulsive disorder is that those who experience it know that the ideas that bother them are crazy, yet they are unable to absolutely, resolutely dismiss them. The ideas take root precisely because you try so hard not to think about them. It's like someone saying don't think about green elephants.

I had always prided myself on an affected anti-intellectualism (hence the interest in dishwashing), but when I found I could no longer think clearly and organically—NORMALLY—it was absolutely horrifying. I realized that all I really had going for me, and all I really valued, was my ability to think. And without that . . . I felt disturbed. I felt ill. Almost instantly, I felt like I had become a crazy person.

I went deeper and deeper into myself. Becoming so distracted and upset that I was unable to carry on a normal conversation—I'm sure I looked obviously distressed to anyone who encountered me—I spent great amounts of time alone, at night, playing pinball, reading novels in all-night diners, hanging out at the 7-11 . . .

By March I felt an inexplicable and steady rage toward everything. I could no longer function, really; I could no longer do what I wanted to do. There was—I was eighteen, after all—an endless amount of sexual energy, if not sexual aggression, that I found no reasonable outlet for. I was still unable to talk to girls without stuttering and being reduced to odd mumbling. My sexual appetite was fed and further twisted by a steady fare of *Penthouse Magazine*, to whose stories and pictures I masturbated daily.

If all this made me feel quasi-suicidal, I never really considered the action; but as the disturbances continued, the notion of suicide was for the first time brought, and then deeply buried, into my daily consciousness. I experienced what I later learned is called "suicidal ideation"—fleeting images and thoughts of suicide. I often saw pictures of myself killing myself, but the ideas never turned into an actual plan. There was never a moment when I said, okay, I'm going to go do it now. I wouldn't allow myself to go there. The one time I got closer than any other I do remember thinking that I could not inflict such a thing on my mother. Instead of turning into a suicidal act, the anger and frustration eventually became directed outward: I began to feel a perpetual rage toward the world generally and other people specifically. I didn't blame others for my predicament (other than, as any eighteen-year-old would, my parents), but I just didn't know where this insanity came from, and why it arose so suddenly. I realized that my family—starting with William and Joseph in the ocean—had been on an upward trajectory of success, an ongoing ascendancy in the world. With a crushing sense of failure, I thought that I was the first of the Barbers to break this unspoken covenant of improvement, the first to fall off the escalator. I compared myself ashamedly to my father, who five decades before had walked along these same paths of Harvard Yard. Unlike me, he had walked with the purposeful march of a scholarship student driven to beat out the preppies of Andover and Exeter—people like me. And he did beat them out. I wasn't, it appeared, measuring up to my father, the varsity letterman in crew and magna cum laude student, whose tenure at Harvard was broken in halves by a world war in which he found himself trooping through the fields of France with a mortar gun, being shot at by Germans. I thought bitterly—in my few moments of clarity that year—that I was in my own war, but of a far different sort. And it never occurred to me to tell anyone about the war, especially my patients. That would have been far too embarassing.

I may as well just say it. I started having thoughts of killing people. By the end of my freshman year, I couldn't go out at night, afraid that if I went out on some April evening, I might—and I saw constant visions of myself compelled to do these things—grab some woman or man, drag them into the bushes, and stab them.

But the crux of it was that—in the surrealism of that year, of sleeplessness, of immaturity, of leaving home for the first time, of constant obsessiveness—I lost over time the ability to distinguish what I had and had not done. The movie, in other words, became real. In that howling storm of thought, I lost the ability to know, FOR SURE, that I had done nothing aggressive. Thoughts that I had hurt other people ate at me all day long. To me they were intolerable.

It got so crazy that I would have to look back at people after I walked past them to make sure I hadn't harmed them. If they were still walking, I knew I hadn't killed them. After a while I couldn't distinguish between what I imagined I had done and what I had actually done, or not done. The endless home movie of me perpetrating violence on others become almost completely real.

To combat the thoughts, I developed a mantra, No Thought No Fear No Action. I would repeat it to myself . . . No Thought No Fear No Action No Thought No Fear No Action No Thought No Fear No Action . . . during an attack of obsessive thoughts. But usually it didn't work. In their place, the violent thoughts usually took over.

Black black

black black black black black black black black black black black black
black black black black black black black black black black black black
black black black black black black black black black black black black
black black black black black black black black black black black black
black black black black black black black black black black black black
black black black black black black black black black black black black
black black black black black black black black black black black black
black black black black black black black black black black black black
black black black black black black black black black black black black
black black black black black black black black black black black black
black black black black black black black black . . .

◦ ◦ ◦

And so it was that sort of mental battlefield I was trying to keep
at bay as Nick and I drove along the black river and then westward
through the New England forest and the roads narrowed and became
less illuminated. Houses or any sign of human settlement or activity
became farther and farther apart. There were fewer radio stations to
choose from. The air, even inside the car, got colder. My ears popped
as we drove steadily uphill on dark, unlit roads. We were silent as we
realized we were in wilder, more alien country, a far different landscape
from the mild and familiar and banal rhythms of Cold River and its
surroundings. We were, in short, out of our territory. I felt awful, as I
always did those days.

Nick broke the silence.

"Spooky, huh?" he said. "I wonder what Al Camus would think about
this." Nick always called him Al. He liked to do that with the names of
intellectuals: John Paul Sartre, Freddy Nietzsche, Hank Thoreau. "Do
you think he could have set *The Stranger* in the Berkshires or what?"

"Yeah, Meursault in the Berkshires," I said.

We pulled off the main road. Following Henry's directions, we drove
through a number of "towns," minute settlements that were more like
thin patches of houses with a store or two. Finally, after the last "town,"
we turned onto a dirt road. This was, Henry had explained over the
phone, the two-mile driveway that led to the farm. We drove in silence,
upward, into the trees.

After five minutes, we appeared to have come to the end. The road simply stopped. Ahead of us there seemed to be the outline of a house, but we couldn't really tell. Everything around us was completely black. All we knew was that we were on top of a great hill, surrounded by an endless black sky and thousands, hundreds of thousands, of trees.

We felt the drop in temperature as soon as we got out of the car. It must have been ten degrees colder here than in Cold River. We looked around as best we could. All was still.

"What's up, dudes?"

I turned around to find Henry's face inches from mine. His typically lurid orange hair almost served as illumination. His face (as I write, its appearance is coming back to me just a little) looked older than before. The lines were etched deeper. He still had his silly nervous smile. He reeked of scotch. I tried to make out, through the darkness, the person I feared I had become.

"Oh, nothing much," I said, as always.

"How the hell are you?" Nick said.

The three of us shook hands in a bizarre formal way, on top of that dark hillside.

"Welcome," Henry said. "Welcome to the Berkshires."

We didn't quite know what to say. We just stood there, the three of us.

"So would you like a tour of the place?" Henry said.

"Sure."

Nick and I took our bags out of the car and walked toward the house.

"No, no, over here." Henry said. He led us through the dark to a small open space away from the house.

"This, over here, is the pond," he said. If we focused hard, we could see the reflection of some moonlight on water.

"And this," Henry said, leading us in a different direction, "this is the lawn." He said this with a certain weightiness, as if there was something terribly profound about what he had said that we were supposed to respond to. We just stood there, barely making out a small patch of grass.

"And over here, these are the woods." He pointed vaguely beyond. I was feeling cold and impatient.

"What about going inside?" I said.

"Okay, if you want to," Henry said, as if that were an awfully irrelevant request.

We walked toward the dark looming structure.

"This is the house," Henry said superfluously. "It's two hundred years old, and my father bought it from a couple of gay guys in the sixties. And they bought it from a farmer."

Through the gloom I examined, as best I could, the classic New England saltbox, painted green with red shutters.

"And the farmer," Henry exclaimed, his voice rising, "hung himself right there!" He pointed to the attic.

I peered upward, trying to look at the attic and feeling an immediate surge of anxiety. I looked through the darkness to get a read on Nick's face, but I couldn't see him well enough. I realized that I was being presented with a number of possibilities. Was Henry making this up? If so, why he was doing it? To taunt us with a ghost story? Or was he trying to tell us he was suicidal? And why did he have to tell us within minutes of our arrival—before we'd even gone into the house?

Having delivered his message, Henry stood in front of us, wild-eyed. I remember that at that specific moment a word entered my mind. That word was *gothic*. Not long ago I looked it up in the dictionary: "Barbarous, crude, relating to a style of art that emphasizes the grotesque, mysterious and desolate." Before this was over, I felt intuitively, I might find myself in something gothic, something out of Hawthorne, or Wagner, or Goethe. I found it soothing to think this. It was helpful to believe that I was in the midst of something not actually real but an imaginative tradition with a larger context than the hillside we were standing on. It made Henry and his obvious oddness—for he seemed to be in even worse shape than usual—seem smaller and more manageable. At least that's what I made myself think.

"Can we bloody go in now?" Nick said. Henry nodded. Finally we entered the house and put down our bags on the wood floor of the front hallway.

"This is the kitchen," Henry said. We were in a large combined kitchen and breakfast room, which was dominated on one side by a brick fireplace and on the other by a beautiful round wooden table, on which sat bottles of scotch and tequila. Henry then led us into the center hallway, pointing out a sparse, dark sitting room, and then took us upstairs.

"Here's your room," he pointed a room out to me, off a long hallway. "I'm across the hall." I entered a spare, clean room with white walls and nothing much in it but a bed and bureau. It was the essence of Puritan minimalism. I deposited my bag and tried not to think about the alleged suicide in the attic above.

"So what are we going to fucking do for food?" Nick said, after we had reconvened in the kitchen. A cursory inspection revealed that there was nothing to eat in the house but sugar and cornflakes.

"Food," Henry said airily. "Food." It seemed an illusory concept for Henry. He gestured vaguely to the round kitchen table, on which sat the cereal.

"What the fuck are we supposed to do," Nick boomed, "eat cornflakes all weekend?"

Henry was silent for a moment and seemed to be considering this as a serious possibility.

"I mean, like, meat, potatoes, ice cream?" Nick said.

Henry seemed rather puzzled by these suggestions.

"Come on, Charlie," Nick said, "let's go get some supplies."

Without another word, we left the house, got into the car, and headed back into "town." I had felt awful all day, and even more awful during our brief time at what I had already come to think of as the gothic house, and the Exxon TigerMart was positively exuberant, almost joyous, compared to the miserable place we had just been. The TigerMart was the undisputed center of action in town, its busy parking lot filled with pickup trucks. Men in deer-hunting garb hung out at the register, talking to the cashier. They lingered over gassing up their vehicles while their girlfriends waited seductively for them in the front seat. Nick and I scouted the aisles for the most substantial food we could find, which turned out to be hot dogs, eggs, white bread, frozen french fries, and white powdered doughnuts. We loaded up on these items and headed, not a little reluctantly, back to the gothic house.

Henry drank more scotch while Nick and I cooked and set the table. Under more-normal circumstances we might have resented Henry's dereliction of his host duties, but neither of us felt that way. We knew that cooking and cleaning were among the few things that we could do for him.

Once we finally sat down, we asked the question on our minds.

"So where the hell did you go after you disappeared?" Nick said. I thought about asking him, indignantly, why he had never bothered to tell me about his plans before he left, but didn't bother. I had come home to the shoddy little house we had briefly shared and found him and his van gone.

"California," Henry said. "And I spent a lot of time in western Canada."

"So how was it?" I said.

"Not bad. Kind of pretty," Henry said, and was promptly silent.

I persevered. "So what did you do out there?"

"Drove around, slept in the car, listened to gospel radio shows. Got beat up once. Drank a lot of bad coffee. Thought about things. You know, got away from it all." That last phrase was uttered with extreme sarcasm, as if in parody of a travel ad. He continued, "Oh yeah, one day my van got a flat. I was pulled over by the side of the road, trying to figure out what to do, and a group of Deadheads drove by. I was sure they would help me, being Deadheads, but they just drove on by. Fucking Deadheads. I always hated Jerry Garcia! And, oh yeah, I think I got a venereal disease." He started laughing.

"Jesus Christ," Nick said. "From a whore?"

"Um . . . could you pass the french fries?" Henry said.

We pressed Henry for details, about the venereal disease in particular and the trip in general, but he didn't divulge anything. I never found out any more of what happened on that trip, but I know it wasn't good. I had visions of Henry driving hundreds on hundreds of miles across Saskatchewan, *Microbe Hunters* on the dashboard. It must have given him a wonderful opportunity to become even more introverted. I was just about to say something about that when Henry, perhaps sensing I was about to become intolerably serious, told a funny, bizarre story about a standoff he'd had with a gang of born-again Christians at some honky-tonk hotel or bowling alley or something.

After dinner, we climbed the stairs to go to bed.

"Good night," I said to Henry and Nick.

"Oh," Henry said. "My father is coming tomorrow. He's coming to make us lunch."

"He's coming all the way here to make us lunch?" Nick said.

"Yeah, and I guess he wants to do some work," Henry said.

⋆ ⋆ ⋆

It was funny about Mr. Court coming, I thought later in bed. Was he coming to check up on Henry? Did he think he was in some kind of danger? I tried not to speculate about such matters any further and instead tried to read the book I'd brought with me, *The Deerslayer* by James Fenimore Cooper. I found, in those days after the onslaught of negative thinking that had begun in Harvard Yard, that small things sometimes distracted me. Innocuous television—the stupider the better—sometimes helped, and the flow of words in a good book sometimes eased the oppression of black black black black. *The Deerslayer* seemed appropriately rustic and historical for the setting, but the language was dense and the story hard to follow. I read to page 3, and then, suddenly feeling overwhelmingly exhausted and sick of the book and everything that had gone on that night, I promptly fell asleep.

Nick told me later that on Saturday morning he woke up early, got his camera, and took a healthy walk up and down the hills around the property. He took photographs of little rocky paths going off into the woods, the small pond—looking cheerful now—and the house.

I woke up a little while later. The house and property were completely transformed from the night before. You could actually see things—the house and yard were now brilliantly illuminated with a warm glow. The creepiness of the night before, and the image of the dead farmer, seemed to have been driven off by the daylight. It was the height of the foliage season, and the landscape was a rush of oranges, greens, yellows, and reds.

I was eating powdered doughnuts at the kitchen table when Nick returned, looking vigorous and energetic. We waited around a while for Henry to get up, but he didn't appear. Finally, we left a note, "Dude: back in a few hours," and drove aimlessly through the woods for a couple of hours.

I have a photograph in front of me that Nick took on that drive.

Nick gave it to me recently, and I keep it in my desk here at the shelter. It's a picture of me, and I am standing in front of a makeshift Baptist church by the side of the highway. It's a prefab building, resembling a large trailer park home, and I am standing in front of a billboard that states in large letters: "YOU CAN'T RUN WITH THE DEVIL AND WALK WITH JESUS." I had asked Nick to pull over when I saw that sign. I am standing with my arms outstretched in a state of mock crucifixion. I look like a rakish hipster—my hair is longish, uncombed; I am wearing a leather vest and a green corduroy jacket, and white jeans with leather boots. I am smiling, irreverently. I look pretty good, in a bedraggled sort of way, but I know that the reason I suddenly asked Nick to pull over and take that picture is that it was an impulsive and unpremeditated move to represent, by way of mock crucifixion, the sheer amount of anguish I was in. That fall, exactly one year after the initial attacks in Harvard Yard, was actually worse. The anguishing and violent thoughts had set in, taken hold, and were now the dominant part of my life. Crazy thoughts—thoughts about a million words going through my mind at the same time, about having a million nervous breakdowns in a second, thoughts about killing people and then not knowing if I'd killed them. They don't make any sense to me now—I don't even understand what they *mean* now—but it was a measure of my desperation that mere ideas like these would produce in me a tremendous horrific pain and throw me into some dark state of oblivion. I remember that in those days when I would wake in the morning, I would feel good, seemingly and apparently NORMAL for perhaps a second or two, and then the onslaught of thought that I had left off thinking about when I'd gone to sleep the night before would inevitably return and I would be shrouded in outright pain again. I can say with absolute certainty that there was nothing about that fall—except for a few moments of bland TV or innocuous reading or masturbation when I could lose myself—that was worth living through. I did not retain hope as much as an obstinate inability to harm myself. I simply decided to endure because there was no other choice.

When Nick and I returned, Henry was awake, sort of, and his father had arrived. Mr. Court was busy making beef stew for us. I wondered again if the purpose of his visit was to check up on his ill son. If so, there was no overt sign of it. He seemed calm and phlegmatic, as always. Maybe he was just doing what he might normally do on a fall Saturday. It would be just like William—the worker, the scholar—to drive three hours to make lunch for us, then work rigorously outside, chopping wood, mowing the lawn, and then implacably drive all the way back to Cold River, without complaint.

I remember nothing of the lunch except that the stew was good (a substantial contrast to TigerMart fare) and that, even around his father, Henry said little. Henry favored his father greatly over his mother—he actually liked his father—but still he was silent. I am sure he felt intimidated by him.

I do recall that at lunch William and I spoke about Vietnam. PBS had come out that fall with a multi-episode documentary on the war, and William and I had both been watching it. Nick and Henry and I could remember little of the war, other than the return of POWs in the early 1970s, and the campus strike at the college in the spring of 1969. One of my first memories (and probably Henry's too) was of the scarlet fists spray-painted on the campus sidewalks, with the word "STRIKE!" underneath imploring students to boycott classes. While William joined the strike and actively protested the war, my father resolutely continued to teach his classes. My father and William were long-term colleagues who maintained a healthy respect and a healthy distance. My father, innately more conservative and almost ten years older, was wary of William Court's increasingly radical politics.

Vietnam transformed William Court. Once a reasonably conventional English professor and college dean, he began to feel, in the chaos of the sixties, that the context in which texts were taught was at least as important as the texts themselves. With the war going on, it was no longer relevant just to teach Shakespeare. You had to look at the context in which you were teaching, and in particular at how that context helped to create a culture that was killing people en masse on the other side of the globe. He turned left. He grew his hair long and started wearing black jeans. He developed a course, "Socialism in America," which was taught in a nonauthoritarian "socialist" manner, with students grading teachers and everybody, of course, being hip and cool and calling each other by their first name. But throughout it all, William retained his essential equanimity and professionalism. Although his beliefs had been turned upside down, his manner never changed. He faced the imploding world in the same imperturbable, straightforward, and undisturbed manner that he always had. Henry told me in his halting way that his mother had become more volatile over the years, perhaps in an attempt to provoke William into some sort of emotional reaction. But it didn't work—overt emotion was simply not an area that William traded in. As a result, William and Joyce were forever changing their arrangements—sometimes they were living together, other times apart, other times they were legally separated. I gave up asking about their status, and Henry didn't want to talk about it anyway.

William worked in the yard after lunch. I offered to help him. He smiled and said that was unnecessary. I didn't push it; something about the way he politely refused made me aware that he really wanted to be alone. William always appeared to be thinking some great thought, and I didn't want to intrude. There was a powerful clarity and lucidity about the things he did and said. My parents had some of his books around the house, scholarly and critical texts published by top university presses. I had read bits and pieces of them even as a teenager, not really understanding any of it, but being aware of the power of the thought and precision of the writing.

᠊ᠥ ᠊ᠥ ᠊ᠥ

I went into the kitchen and watched out the window while Henry joined William in the field. Henry looked soft and tentative compared to his father. I watched William work and Henry stand by passively, and I wondered whether the problem with Henry and me was that we were just soft. Maybe the difficulty with Henry and me, I considered, was that we just weren't hungry enough. We'd been given everything, whereas William and my father, despite their later differences, had shared a hunger to get away from the drabness and limitations of their upbringings. My Dad had fought tooth and nail to get out of the dustbowl of Depression-era Kansas, and he had succeeded by winning a scholarship to Harvard, then a Rhodes scholarship to Oxford. William similarly had abandoned the conventions of his oil executive father and the Midwest of his boyhood and gone to college at Oberlin and completed a PhD at Harvard, immersing himself in a new rich world of ideas that he loved. Whatever their political and stylistic differences, my father and Mr. Court both shared a joyful intellectual workaholicism. I could picture William Court getting up at 3 a.m. to write down an idea that had just occurred to him, as my father was wont to do in the middle of the night.

After a productive afternoon of feeding us and taking care of his property, William stated rather abruptly that he needed to be off. He said a good-bye to Henry, Nick, and me that was both stiff and warm, then got into his car and drove off. He couldn't have known that that was the last time he would see his son. No, my guess is that, calmly I'm sure, he thought mainly about literary theory all the way back to Cold River.

◆ ◆ ◆

The house seemed palpably less stable with his departure. Henry turned to me. "Wanna go for a drive?" he said.

"Sure," I said, for what else was there to do?

It was getting dark—just the time for Henry to start the day.

"Okay," I said. I went to get Nick, who was sleeping in his room.

The van had no side windows and no rear seats. This left the third passenger (Nick and I took turns) to sit on the floor in the back of van, getting tossed about, as Henry took wide turns on the mountain roads. He drove aggressively, but inconsistently so, gunning the engine and then hitting the brakes with no apparent pattern or regularity. Within minutes of sitting in the back, I became nauseated. Henry smoked and listened to his homemade punk tapes as we drove, at a volume that forced the three of us not to talk. The front had the advantage of at least having a seat and some minor visibility afforded by streetlights, but it brought you in closer contact with Henry and his grim vibes. The trip had the ostensible quality of being a tour—every once in a while Henry would gesture to some shadowy landmark as we sped by. For some odd reason, Nick and I didn't complain. Nick, usually so outspoken, sank into glum silence. Henry remained fixed on the relentless driving, smoking cigarette after cigarette, concentrating on the lugubrious music, all as if he were adhering to some deeply obscured interior agenda.

After an hour I had to pee. Henry pulled the van over, annoyed. I seemed to be upsetting his schedule. I got out of the van to discover that we were way up in the hills and that we were right in the middle of the central quad of a college. Next to the bush on which I was peeing was a large placard announcing the name of the college and the very early year of its founding. As a senior at Andover, I had thought about applying to this college. Instead of peeing on a bush, I might have been studying organic chemistry or English literature, or spending time with fully functional friends. I might have been normal. I knew students enrolled at the college now. With a kind of automatic disdain, I thought of them—I imagined them as pre-med and pre-law, suck-ups, brownnosers, probably getting drunk at some frat party, spewing lines to girls in order to get laid.

I looked over at the van, its engine still running, the muffled sound of punk music emanating from its cabin. Through the van's steamy windows I could see the silhouettes of Henry and Nick, lit by the glow of Henry's cigarette. Despite all the facts in front of me—that this trip was idiocy, that I was nauseated and disgusted, that Henry was clearly ill and hopeless, and Nick was impatient and moody—I took a curious pride in my friends. Despite the nausea, the cigarettes, the bad music, the dread that surrounded Henry, I wanted to be with my friends. Nick and Henry more accurately reflected me than the persona that people thought I was, the persona that had gotten me into Harvard.

"How was the peeing?" Nick said when I got back into the van.

"Excellent," I said.

～ ～ ～

More jiggling black. We drove for another hour through the nauseous night. Henry drove more recklessly than ever, braking and accelerating almost randomly, and swerving so hard around turns that Nick and I had to hold on to the sides of the van to keep our balance. It is unclear to me whether Henry knew how uncomfortable he was making us, or whether this was just his idea of a good time. Now I think that his intentions were at least partially sadistic.

We persuaded Henry to make a stop, at a bar in a small town. It was bright and cheerful, like an English pub, and filled with college students happily chatting and drinking. We drank Rolling Rock. Henry said he was thinking of finding work at a restaurant in town, maybe even this restaurant, and he was looking around for a band to play bass in. We looked at the girls, but didn't once think to talk to them. They were distant objects. If one of them by some miracle had come to our table, we wouldn't have known what to say to her. Our pseudowit would have dried up on the spot.

We returned to the farm after another nauseating hour in the van. Nick hopped out of the van and angrily slammed its door.

"Well, that was a lot of fun," he said, marching toward the house. "Good night. You two have a good evening."

Henry seemed surprised, and almost hurt.

"You don't want some scotch?" he said.

"No! And no hot dogs or doughnuts either," Nick said.

"What's his problem?" Henry said to me, with a wry, nervous smile at the edge of his lips.

"I don't know," I said.

Nick having gone to bed, Henry and I drank the scotch. It produced a nice warm feeling. Henry seemed happier than he'd been all weekend. I think that nighttime was the least painful time of the day for him — perhaps because he knew he could sleep soon and wouldn't have to endure being awake for too much longer.

Showing an unusual burst of energy, Henry even made a fire. We sat near it and felt the crackle of the flames. For the first time all weekend, the house felt warm. I remember distinctly that he played George Harrison's first solo album, *All Things Must Pass*. Henry had a sort of George Harrison fetish. He collected all of Harrison's albums, even the mediocre ones, and he protected them carefully. None of them were ever endangered in the trashings. I guess it's not surprising, the George Harrison thing. Henry would have been interested in the most oblique and introverted of the Beatles.

Instead of our nontalk, I wish that I had told Henry about my own ongoing sense of bleakness. I wish I had explained to him that my inner life was not so different from his.

In other words, I desperately wish that I had told him about:

Black, black, black, black, black, black, black, black, black, black, black

and

No thought, No fear, No action; No thought, No fear, No action.

Of all people, Henry would have understood.

I should have just told him the story of my own madness. Maybe he wouldn't have felt so terrible about himself. He still thought I was intact and untroubled. If I had told him, he would have been surprised and maybe heartened, and he might even have told me about his inner disturbances and . . . Who knows? I might have given him some relief from his pain.

Actually, it's more than that. I know I could have helped him. I don't dare think that I could have kept him alive, or saved him from his imminent self-destruction, but I do think that I could have delayed it, or softened it, or something . . . I don't know what exactly. At the very least, he would have been surprised.

Or maybe not. Maybe, and this is something that occurred to me only very recently, maybe Henry knew exactly what was going on with me, sensed it with that powerful intellect. Maybe that's why he sought me out, and why he made the advance that was shortly to follow.

I seem to think that we drank a lot of scotch. After a while, George Harrison stopped singing. Who knows what time it was. My head was pleasantly spinning.

"I'm gonna go to bed, too, man," I said.

"I'll stay up a little while," Henry said.

"See ya in the morning?"

"Or the afternoon." He gave one of his pained smiles.

I went up the creaky stairs to my bedroom. I probably read a page or two of my Fenimore Cooper, feeling again it was a good thing to do—to read James Fenimore Cooper in the woods—but after a couple of pages it seemed too hard to follow. I turned out the light and gratefully fell asleep.

I was disturbed some time later by a tap on the door.

I got up, annoyed, and fumbled my way through the darkness. I opened the door to find Henry standing in front of me, reeling. I don't know how much time had passed, but Henry must have drunk quite a lot more alcohol since I had last seen him. He was visibly drunk, almost teetering in the doorway. His characteristic strange, nervous smile came to his lips.

"I'm sorry to bother you."

"No problem," I said fuzzily.

He moved close, crowding me. He drew his face inches from mine.

"Charlie, I was wondering . . . You've always, umm, always been a good friend to me . . . you know, kind . . . I was wondering . . . could I kiss you?"

"No," I said, immediately. A knee-jerk response.

It was hard to process what he had just said. Had he really asked me to kiss him? I was embarrassed. Had Nick heard us? No, no, no, of course I would say no.

Henry appeared immediately defeated. He paused for a second, and then uttered, "Umm . . . then, could I hug you?"

I considered this for a second or two. "Yes," I said.

And then in that moment Henry placed his arms around me, and I suppose I put my arms around him, and we stood there for I don't know how long, hugging drunkenly in that doorway. He reeked of liquor. We might have stood there for seconds, or it might have been minutes. I don't know how long it was. After an uncertain period of time Henry withdrew his arms, turned around, and slunk back into the darkness. And I went back to bed not quite believing what had just happened. I did not sleep well.

I awoke early, more disturbed than usual. Nick and I ate a hurried breakfast. We polished off the last of the Hostess powdered doughnuts.

"Do you wanna go?" I said.

"Yeah," he said.

We had planned to stay well into Sunday, but I know we were both thinking the same thing: What's the point of staying around? More nauseating trips in the van? More pissing in the dark? More listening to the Dead Kennedys and George Harrison? More sleeping until noon? Even though I hadn't told Nick what had happened in the middle of the night, I could tell he wanted to get out of there as much as I did.

We trudged back up the stairs to say good-bye to our friend. We stood over him in his bed.

"Henry . . . ," Nick said. "Henry . . ."

He didn't stir.

"Henry . . . ," I tried.

He didn't move.

"We're leaving," I said.

Finally Nick shook him. "Henry. We're leaving."

He sort of moved and made brief eye contact with us, then looked away. He looked pallid and awful. He was sweating.

"What's up?" he said, as if we were meeting casually on a street corner.

"We're taking off a little early," I said by way of explanation. Henry didn't look at me.

"Oh. Okay . . . sure," he said.

Awkward silence.

"We can make our own way out. You don't have to get up or anything," I said.

"Oh. Okay." Henry said.

"Thanks for the weekend," I said.

"Yeah, thanks," Nick said.

"Oh, yeah. Sure. No problem," Henry said. We attempted to shake his hand. A pale hand arose from the covers. We shook it. Once again, it was all oddly formal, surreal.

"See ya," Nick and I said.

"See ya," Henry said.

Just before we walked out the door, Nick turned around and said vehemently, and with an obvious passion, "Henry, why don't you get the hell out of here and come back to Cold River and be with us?"

Henry considered this for a few moments. "Because every time I think about going back to Cold River, I just want to get drunk," he said.

We walked out the door. "Drunk" would be the last word.

·�· ·�· ·�·

The bad feeling pervaded the trip home.

I slowly realized how angry I was at Henry. I suppose I recognized the kiss as a desperate thing, but all I could think was that Henry had put me in a spot, forced me into an awkward position. He'd brought our friendship into . . . homosexual territory.

Well, fuck you, Henry. Fuck you. Keep your arms and your lips to yourself. What Henry and I and Nick did, what we always did, was talk about nothing and do nothing and drive around and listen to music and drink, and in one moment he'd changed all that. He'd broken the code of silence. What was I supposed to do now?

I looked out on the highway, which was getting flatter and wider, at the malls starting to pop up, and the land evening out, and I thought about telling Nick about the encounter. Finally I told him the story with a kind of angry relish.

"Jesus Christ, I don't know whether to laugh or cry," Nick said.

"Me neither," I said.

"I didn't know he was gay," Nick said.

"I don't know that he is gay," I said.

"Who fucking knows," Nick said.

"I mean bisexual maybe," I said.

"He was probably just drunk out of his mind. I tell you one thing, I wouldn't have fucking kissed him," Nick said.

We drove on.

"Why do you think he didn't ask to kiss me?" Nick said, half-serious, half-joking.

"I think he knew you'd have punched him in the nose," I said. For the first time, we laughed.

We drove toward Cold River and home.

⚬ ⚬ ⚬

"Mother?"

I was in my parents' home.

"Mother?"

There was no sign of her in the house. I looked outside. My mother was in our wide yard, on top of the hill, reading. It was much hotter in Cold River than it had been in the mountains. The grass was scorched-looking, white. Strawlike. She had half a cup of tea nestled in the grass at her side. It glinted in the sun. She smiled at me, cheerful as ever.

"How was the weekend?"

I tried to smile. "Oh, great," I said.

"What did you do?" she said.

"Oh, not much. Drove around, as usual."

"Oh." She understood, implicitly knowing that Henry could not have been much of a host.

There was a pause.

"Would you like some tea? And ginger cookies? I think there are some left."

I didn't hear her.

"Would you like some tea? And ginger cookies?"

"Sure . . . Thanks, I'll get it."

"No, no, I'll get it," she said.

And so my mother got up and walked through the strawlike grass and I watched her walking. I took her chair and looked at the line of sassafras trees at the bottom of our yard. In five minutes she returned with tea and four ginger cookies on a blue and white saucer. I ate them. The mood dictated that we talk no more of the weekend.

"How's the Stendahl?" I said.

"Oh, wonderful. I reread *Le rouge et le noir*."

"Are you reading it in French or English?"

"Oh, English. I'm afraid my French is a little out of practice . . . How was your weekend?" she tried again.

"Oh, fine."

"How was Henry?" I noticed she had a hard time even saying his name. "Fine . . . well, okay," I said.

My mother didn't press further.

And so I stood in the middle of the field filled with straw. The sun seemed blindingly white. As we talked more about Stendahl and drank our tea, everything became more and more white. The field became luminous. The tea, the blue and white saucers, the straw, the sun, my hand, my mother's hair, her smile: everything turned brighter and brighter, until I could see nothing but a blinding field of white light.

our

The Weight of Spoons

Eight days later, on a Monday morning, I was reading over the weekend's football scores in the newspaper when the telephone rang.

It was Nick. His voice was different. He was crying.

"Charlie, did you hear?"

"No," I said.

"I just got a call from William Court," he said. "Henry killed himself up at the farm."

"What?" I heard myself say.

"Henry killed himself up at the farm . . . The motherfucker." Nick was sobbing.

"Jesus Christ," I said. I sat down. I felt my grip loosen on the telephone. I felt kicked in the stomach. I felt once again that immediate infusion of acid into the depths of my intestines.

"How?" I said.

"He asphyxiated himself. He suffocated himself somehow in the van . . . with the exhaust. I don't know, I guess he rigged up some hose and rerouted the van's exhaust back into the cabin."

"When did it happen?" I felt foolish asking these practical questions; they didn't matter, all that mattered was that he was dead.

"William found his body yesterday. He might have done it a couple of days ago."

"I can't believe he fucking did it," I said.

"Oh, I can." Nick said, just slightly more composed now. "The poor motherfucker . . ."

I couldn't imagine Henry not being alive. I tried to see him as no longer moving. I couldn't see him that way. Even in his compromised, troubled state he had been talking, drinking, joking—and of course, trying to kiss me—just a week ago.

It hit me . . . Trying to kiss me . . . could that have made a difference? Could I have made a difference?

Nick said, "Do you think he asked us up as a way to say good-bye?"

"I don't know. I don't know," I said, speaking very softly. "How would I know?"

I didn't want to talk anymore.

"Nick, I'll call you later. In an hour."

"Okay."

"Are you okay?" I said.

"No," he said.

I hung up the phone and moved slowly. I recall in those moments moving very slowly in everything I did. I had a feeling of looking at myself from above. I saw myself go to the couch and lie down. I saw myself get up again after a while, go get some blankets, lie down again, and shut my eyes. I saw myself stay there for most of the next couple of days.

Unlike Nick, I didn't cry. I never have cried over Henry's death. (Perhaps if I had, I wouldn't have needed to write a book about it.)

It didn't seem real. But then again, nor was I shocked, really. Of course I was at first, but then everything was just numbness. And then after a long period of numbness, came the feeling, the slow and profound realization, that things had changed. The earth under my feet would never feel as solid; the links between us all could shatter at any time. And then it was numbness again. And then it was upset, and then it was deep and almost unbearable upset and fear. All I wanted to do was go to sleep.

Jesus, Henry, why? Why now? Couldn't you have told us what you were planning? Couldn't you have waited it out a little longer? Did you have to do it?

Slowly, I came to understand that Henry had done something awful. Something that he should not have been allowed to do. A crime against nature and the order of things, defying convention and provoking us all—as Henry was wont to do—disturbing and muddying the waters, indefinitely. So the suicide hadn't been so clean after all. But then at other times I felt he did what he had the perfect right to do, and it made perfect sense given the pain he was in.

Yes, I freaked out there on the couch. I sweated; I had difficulty breathing, alternately breathing hard and then gasping for breath; I didn't want to be awake, or alive. I went through great panics. He had tried to kiss me. I'd rebuffed him. Nick and I had left afterward at the first opportunity. We—I—had let him hang. How did that make him feel? What was it like when he woke up later that day, probably late in the afternoon, hungover, feeling completely abandoned? Was that the moment when he made up his mind? Had I . . . had we . . . contributed to his death? Had I killed him?

Should I have kissed him? Should I have hugged him, had sex with him, given him whatever he wanted? Would that have made a difference? By not kissing him, what did I do? I tried to wrap my mind around these questions, and in anxiety gave up after I couldn't think about them anymore. But I thought about these questions, for weeks, and months. They became my obsessive loops of thought, side by side with all the other OCD material mucking up my brain.

When my parents came home at dinnertime the day Nick called, I tried to act fully composed when I told them about Henry's death. They had already heard the news on campus. They had tried to call me, but I hadn't picked up the phone. My mother and father were shocked and duly sympathetic. They were upset for Henry's parents. My mother said to me, "Your father and I knew someone at Oxford who killed himself. He was also young, and intelligent. It was very sad."

My mother's words were meant to comfort, but they only angered me. It was as if she were saying there was a precedent for what had happened. In my state of confusion, I at least wanted to think that what I was going through was unique—that a suicide had never happened before, at least not one quite like this, in the history of the world. That nobody else had felt what I was feeling. It was as if my mother was saying that Henry's death was somehow respectable, that there was an Old World antecedent for such behavior. But I didn't say any of that. I just nodded.

That night, Nick and I met up and went for a long soggy walk around the campus. It was just like the old days; we walked in circles. We walked in the same circles that we used to walk with Henry. It was pitch-dark. We could have gone somewhere light and dry to talk, but it didn't seem right. There seemed no more fitting tribute to Henry than to walk around the campus in the dark and the rain.

When Nick and I met that evening, we didn't hug, and we didn't say "how awful." Nor did we say "I'm sorry," or "It was his choice and we need to respect it." We didn't say what everybody else said to each other. There was no need to. I don't think we said all that much to each other in the rain.

But we did talk about why. Actually it was not so much why, but why *now*. Without ever talking about it, we knew that Henry had been ready to pick himself off at any time. Had the weekend been a planned farewell? Had it been as choreographed, in its own way, as the trashings or the placement of *Microbe Hunters* on the dashboard? We talked about the mysterious trip to California and the West. "You know what I think?" Nick said. "I think he realized then that his problems weren't going to go away. When he set out, as the Microbe Hunter, he might have believed that if he went to a different place, his problems would go away. When they didn't, or got worse, that's when he decided to come back East to kill himself."

I didn't disagree. I think we both felt that the whole thing was planned, but we couldn't quite bring ourselves to say it. It still bothers me.

Nick and I speculated about Henry's body. Mr. Court must have had to make the arrangements. I imagined Henry in a morgue somewhere in Massachusetts. A cold, quiet morgue.

⋄ ⋄ ⋄

Henry's funeral was on an unusually warm day a month later in the college chapel. It was early December, and it must have been close to sixty degrees. The delay in scheduling the funeral resulted, of course, from everybody's shock but also, I imagine, from the difficulty in finding an appropriate, dignified way to put Henry to rest.

Mrs. Court was from an Irish Catholic family, and in the brief time I'd spent with her, I sensed that she was fitfully religious. But after Henry died, she became fervently Catholic. She enlisted a priest, I'm not sure from where, to preside over the service.

Nick, Sam—who was back from India, where he had lived for a

couple of years after high school—and I were the ushers. We met outside the chapel a half hour before the ceremony. Nick wore a pinstripe suit—certainly the first time I had seen him so attired—and I had dug out an old suit of my father's. Sam, still tanned from the years in India, arrived at the event wearing a pink tuxedo. He wore a fuchsia jacket and pink trousers with black stripes, and black sneakers.

"What the hell are you up to?" Nick said, sounding both annoyed and impressed.

Sam smiled. "It's a celebration, man. A celebration of Henry's life."

But it's more than that, I thought. There was an edge to Sam's costume, and to his voice. Sam was pushing back. In his mind, Henry had inflicted an absurd and hurtful act on us all, and Sam was going to wear an absurd costume to acknowledge the sheer meanness of Henry's choice. I understood, but I couldn't muster any anger toward Henry. A few weeks later, at a bar, Sam confirmed his anger toward Henry. "He could have gone on," Sam told me. "He could have survived. He just gave UP!" And what did you ever do to help him, I thought. And then I stopped. For what had I ever done to help him?

I was surprised to see that there were about 150 people in attendance. It was a diverse crowd. The great majority of those attending were colleagues of Henry's parents at the college, who were there only out of a forlorn sense of duty. My parents were there, as were probably half the entire faculty above a certain age. Most of those present, including the priest, had never known Henry. But that was okay—it was clear that, except for the eulogy that Mr. Court was going to deliver, the ceremony was not at all about Henry.

A minority of those paying their respects were various murky friends and associates of Henry's. There were friends of Henry's from the restaurant, a couple of friends of ours from high school, and a few especially disreputable-looking types that I suspected Henry knew from his drug travels. I had never met or seen any of the druggy types. Henry had kept that side of his life separate.

Henry's sister was there. She had returned from I don't know where—I think she may have been living in New Zealand. She was perhaps five years older than Henry, and I hardly knew her. I had pretty much forgotten she existed. She was never around when we were growing up and must have left home at a young age. I didn't recognize her at first; in the great Henry Court tradition she had dyed pink hair and, I think, a nose ring. She looked beautiful, and awful.

Nick escorted Mrs. Court into the church and seated her in the front row. I sat my parents in a row somewhere in the middle. Nick said later that he feared that Mrs. Court would go into some epileptic fit precipitated by dread and horror. He was amazed and relieved to have gotten her seated in the pew without incident. Nick and I were aware from the start that Mrs. Court might never fully recover from the blow. For all her oddities, one thing everybody knew about Mrs. Court was that she was passionate about everything she involved herself with, whether it was English literature, alcohol, or her son. This very passion had turned Henry away. But you knew, we all knew, that she would feel his death—this probable rejection of her and everything she believed in—with a passion of the most negative, and possibly most destructive, sort.

Of course, in Catholic tradition suicide is a mortal sin. The priest did not address the reason for Henry's death, but seemed to place great emphasis on the need for "God's forgiveness of sins." He delivered an earnest workmanlike eulogy, and he seemed viscerally relieved when he was done.

"Henry was in a lot of pain for a long, long time." I distinctly remember that's how Mr. Court began his eulogy, or speech, or whatever it was, about Henry. (He wrote me not long ago that was not at all how he began it. Such is memory.) It remained to him to address the nature of Henry's death. He explained that death had always been near Henry, that as a child, he had twice nearly died from serious illnesses. This was news to me; Henry had never spoken about any of it. The speech was, in effect, an explanation of the amount of pain that Henry had been in, and a defense of Henry's unquestioned right to take his life to get rid of that pain. In his recent letter to me, Mr. Court said that he hadn't planned to rationalize Henry's death, but the "priest had pissed me off with all that sin stuff." But what I recall is not so much what he said, but how he said it: Mr. Court was clear-eyed, strong, and unapologetic. He didn't lose his composure once. I felt very close to him as he spoke. I don't know why exactly. My contacts with him had been quick and somewhat superficial, but there, in the chapel, I responded to his enormous sense of clarity. He was wonderfully, exquisitely clear.

He knew what happened. He explained what happened. He explained how he saw it. He was able to stand up in front of everybody. He showed that he was able to function in the midst of it. Sure, it was oddly dry and removed. I suppose it had about it the feel of a textual exegesis. But that was Mr. Court's nature. What did we expect him to do, beat his chest and tear his hair out? I didn't care how he arrived at his stability—the thing was that he got there. He retained, in other words, the ability to function.

A much smaller group assembled for the burial afterward. As Henry's coffin was being placed in the ground in that corner of the graveyard closest to the Dunkin' Donuts, and a group of about thirty of us soberly stood and watched, a great black bird flew across the sky. Nick and I were standing toward the back of the group. "What the fuck is that?" said the man next to us, an English professor who was the world's greatest expert on Laurence Sterne or somebody like that. The three of us watched the unidentifiable great beast—it seemed part crow, part raven, part vulture—fly into the strangely warm afternoon air. After the ceremony, Nick and I went on one of our campus walks. Independently we had both come to the conclusion that the great fucking disturbing bird had been the spirit of Henry, presiding over the ludicrous spectacle.

The night of the funeral I had tea with Sam and his father, Tony, the poet in residence. The Blakes were fun, theatrical people, full of life and humor.

Tony was indignant about the suicide. "I've had bad weeks, even bad months, when life was not particularly pleasant, or even worth living. But suicide? Never. He was young and handsome and clever. I mean, it makes you feel the world is just one big funeral pyre." He shook his body, as if trying to throw off the horror of the day.

"But wasn't Mr. Court's composure during the eulogy remarkable?" I said.

"I couldn't believe it," said Tony, indignantly. "It was perverse. If it had been my bloody son, you can be damn sure that I wouldn't have been so fucking composed."

The Blakes held a flamboyant annual New Year's Eve party. In our circles, it was the social event of the year. All the interesting people in Cold River went, from the manager of the town dump to some of the town's wealthiest families. That year's party, held a few weeks after the funeral, was held in honor of Henry Court. Sam and Tony placed a picture of Henry (how they were able to locate a picture of him, I don't know) on the front door and put a sign up asking that everybody remember his spirit. We all agreed that drinking to oblivion seemed a much more fitting tribute to Henry than any Catholic eulogy by a priest that never knew him.

Some months after the funeral a Letter to the Editor appeared in the Cold River newspaper. The letter addressed American policy toward Cuba and was sympathetic to the Cubans. It was signed by William Court.

"Isn't it funny, that he's writing about this?" I said to my mother. "I mean, who cares about Castro when his son has died?"

My mother said, "It's what he needs to do now. It's a sign that he's getting back to normal."

᛫ ᛫ ᛫

In the days and nights after the suicide, I began to find some tranquillity in unexpected things. Things like objects.

I spent great amounts of time looking at objects. Until that point I had taken very little account of the physical things that exist in the world. I'd never really noticed them. Typically I was always thinking, usually about things of no consequence, but thinking nonetheless. I, and Henry, and my parents, and Henry's parents, and pretty much everyone I knew, lived exclusively in the mental sphere.

But now, in the quiet of my parents' house in the weeks after Henry's death, I contemplated things as they were. I looked at shoes and pears and spoons and tangerines and cardboard. I looked at the shapes of things, the curve of wine bottles and onions and carved wood. I looked at details—the hundreds of miniature dimples on the surface of an eggshell, like on skin, and the hundreds of miniature white spots that you see if you look closely at a Red Delicious apple.

I also spent great amounts of time examining text. Not books or magazines—nothing momentous like that. Mainly I read product labels—the contents of toothpaste and shampoos, the ingredients of brownies. I read classified ads for hours about things for sale, apartments for rent, cats and dogs to adopt. Nothing was more enjoyable—therapeutic, even—than reading the directions on the back of an antacid carton.

To me, no American writer wrote better about mental vulnerability (or "emotional bankruptcy," as he called it) than F. Scott Fitzgerald. In his last broken-down years, when he was saturated with alcohol and scorched from trooping his wife in and out of mental hospitals, Fitzgerald wrote poetically, rapturously even, about his "crack-up," and the crack-ups of others. One of his last short stories was "The Lost Decade," about a former architect who is making a reentry into the world after a disappearance of ten years spent in drunken oblivion. Trimble, the architect, is at lunch at a fine restaurant in midtown Manhattan with a young, enthusiastic magazine editor, Orrison, whose task it is to reorient him to the world. After lunch, Orrison offers to give Trimble a tour of the shining new skyscrapers that have arisen in midtown during Trimble's decade-long disappearance. They stand outside the restaurant:

> "From here you get a good candid focus on Rockefeller Center," [Orrison] pointed out with spirit "—and the Chrysler Building and the Armistead Building, the daddy of all the new ones."
>
> "The Armistead Building," Trimble rubber-necked obediently. "Yes—I designed it."
>
> Orrison shook his head cheerfully—he was used to going out with all kinds of people. . . .
>
> He paused by the brass entablature in the cornerstone of the building. "Erected 1928," it said.
>
> Trimble nodded.
>
> "But I was taken drunk that year—every-which-way drunk. So I never saw it before now."
>
> "Oh." Orrison hesitated. "Like to go in now?"
>
> "I've been in it—lots of times. But I've never seen it. And now it isn't what I want to see. I wouldn't ever be able to see it now. I simply want to see how people walk and what their clothes and shoes and hats are made of. And their eyes and hands. . . .
>
> "What do you want to see most?" Orrison asked. . . .
>
> Trimble considered.
>
> "Well—the backs of people's heads," he suggested. "Their

necks—how their heads are joined to their bodies. I'd like to hear what those two little girls are saying to their father. Not exactly what they're saying but whether the words float or submerge. . . ."

"The weight of spoons," said Trimble, "so light. A little bowl with a stick attached. The cast in that waiter's eye. I knew him once but he wouldn't remember me." . . .

It was all kind of nutsy, Orrison decided. . . .

That's just the way I felt, that's all I wanted to do, all that I was capable of doing at the time: feel the weight of spoons. Spoons and bowls and melons and the text of the classified section, all these were enormously soothing, affirming. They brought solace. They were neutral—they were not going to self-destruct and disappear.

I was reduced—or elevated perhaps—to feeling the weight of spoons. Yes, elevated. Elevated to feeling the weight of spoons. It felt good to think no more but simply to coexist with the world of objects.

᛫᛫ ᛫᛫ ᛫᛫

I resolutely, consciously, told myself that Henry's suicide did not make me suicidal. I had heard about copycat suicides, and I rejected that idea firmly. If Henry died, why should I die? Of course I was thinking the same anguished thoughts, the same loopy thoughts of words repeating and violent urges and crazy ideas that I had since Harvard Yard, and now I had the additional guilt and sense of fragility induced by Henry's death, but I was not going to succumb to them.

Shortly after Henry died, I was driving with a friend on a road I'd driven on hundreds of times. Jim was a friend from another circle of acquaintances; he didn't know Henry or Nick. Randolph Road went down a hill and intersected with a rural highway. At the intersection was a blinking red light.

Instead of stopping at the flashing light, I accelerated.

"What the hell are you doing, Charlie?" shouted Jim.

Before I could react, we had passed through the intersection at sixty miles an hour. If a car or truck had been going along that highway, surely Jim and I would have died.

"What the fuck is wrong with you?" Jim said.

I didn't answer. "I'm sorry," I said, uselessly.

"You could have killed us!" Jim said.

"I'm sorry," I said again.

·❦· ·❦· ·❦·

Perhaps it all came down to a purple shirt.

A few days after I almost killed Jim on Randolph Road, I was in a clothing store, deciding whether or not to buy a shirt. I was in an odd mood. The store was large and warehouselike, and the piped-in music was loud and unsettling. I picked the shirt off the rack—it was a purple canvas Levi's shirt. The usual considerations ran through my mind—did it fit? could I afford it? did I want to afford it?—when it struck me . . . why buy the shirt at all? There's a good chance you might not be around in a few weeks or months. You may not even be alive to wear it.

Listening to these last thoughts, I was just about to put the shirt back on the rack and walk away, when I thought: you have to decide whether to buy the shirt or not. It's one or the other. You have to take a stand.

Fuck it, I thought, I need to buy the shirt. I don't care if I can't afford it, I don't care if I don't like it, I don't care if it's the ugliest, silliest, most ridiculous looking shirt in the world—I need to buy it.

I need to buy it.

I bought the shirt.

part two

Travels in the Interior

five

Traps, and How to Get Out of Them

I was leaving the store a few minutes after buying the purple shirt when on the sidewalk I ran into friends from Wilson, Bill and Laura. Bill and Laura were hip, interesting students, a striking couple, and Bill had known Henry a little and been kind to him. Bill had been a waiter at the Mexican restaurant where Henry and I had been busboys. Bill was an older student—he'd been in the army for five years before college—and he was a playwright and former trombonist in a disco band. He and I had spent many an evening walking, driving around, talking about Raymond Carver, Eugene O'Neill, Miles Davis, etc. Laura was artsy and dark-eyed and dark-haired, intense and pretty. Once when Bill didn't show up, Laura and I had coffee in the off-campus apartment they shared. I drew her cartoons of the slovenly state of my bedroom (with its various piles of books, papers, unwashed laundry, old coffee cups), and she had laughed. Laura and Bill's apartment, in contrast, was immaculate and filled with little curiosities—figurines, old glass, old photographs—that Laura collected, reminding me of Henry's penchant for hoarding quirky objects. Laura was studying psychology and photography, and she also worked for the local newspaper as a freelance photographer. You could always pick out her pictures in the paper: even if they were of the Labor Day parade on Main Street, her images were closer to those of Robert Frank or something that should be in a gallery in New York than anything that belonged in a local newspaper.

Clutching the bag with the purple shirt to my chest, I said, "It's too bad about Henry." The banality of my words echoed in my ears.

They looked puzzled.

"You heard about Henry," I said. It was more a statement than a question. I assumed the whole world knew about Henry. After all, he had died two weeks ago. It turned out they hadn't heard, so I told them the whole sordid tale of the weekend visit and his death, leaving out only the pass made at me. Bill was silent the entire time I spoke, and looked considerably paler by the time I finished; Laura had begun to cry.

"Did you know Henry?" I asked her.

"No," she said, barely audibly.

Then why are you crying? I thought. I knew him better than just about anybody—that is, about as well as anybody could ever know a person like Henry—and I hadn't (and still haven't) shed a tear over his death. So why the hell are you crying, I thought, both annoyed and impressed by her ability to cry. But I didn't say any of that. We all just stood there on the sidewalk.

There was nothing left to say. Bill and then Laura reached out to embrace me. Up close, holding Laura for a minute, I saw the run of the tears on her cheek. I couldn't believe how thin and delicate her bones were.

After that, whenever I felt particularly bad—which was often—I would think about clutching Laura and feeling the extraordinary delicateness of her body.

⋄ ⋄ ⋄

I pulled the car over on the side of the country road and walked out into a cornfield. I stood in the field of snow in the middle of the night. The exquisite beauty of it was that there was no reason for me to be there. I looked around and noticed snowflakes swirling around me. It was a bitter, exhilarating chill, and I felt myself rise up, tumbling into the sky. From above, the world was as it had not been in years: clear, solid, possibly euphoric. I felt myself go farther up into the snowy air. It got colder outside, but everything sharp and harsh within me melted. Nothing was painful anymore, not even my dark thoughts.

For some reason, one fine brilliant January day—probably a week after I ran into Bill and Laura on the street—the ocd thoughts just stopped. They simply stopped! I was walking through the Wilson campus when . . . poof! . . . they were gone. The loops of thought that had been plaguing me—I can't remember what they were exactly, repeated words, violent thoughts, guilt and misery over Henry, all mixed together—all just seemed to evaporate. It happened in a moment, for no apparent reason. I would think the thoughts, even try to summon them up, and what on the previous day (the previous hour, the previous minute!) had made my heart race and my fists tighten simply didn't hurt anymore. They had dissolved and melted, like the wicked Witch of the West. Their evil tentacles could no longer reach me.

I spent that day in a state of pure effervescence and giddy relief. I don't remember what I did, but it was a day of almost spiritual celebration, a day of rising into ether, a day of slow realizations that a precious and wholly unexpected gift had been delivered to me, an unspeakably precious gift of armor that made me suddenly impervious to everything that had tormented me since those days walking through Harvard Yard. It was a day that made me believe in God. From now on, I was going to be unstoppable! Untouchable! I had seen the worst, and faced it down. My friend had died. I had survived, and I had moved through despair and knifelike thoughts and they were over and I was delivered and now I was going to have a brilliant extreme life and become a great writer or whatever the hell it was I was going to do, and most critically, these horrible obsessive thoughts were never going to bother me again. Tears of joy and oblivion! From now on, until my death at age ninety-four as a happy, loved, famous, wealthy man, doting wife and children at my side in a great mansion on a hill, I was going to be clean and free of all pathos and poisonous thoughts. Breathing was ecstasy!

Shoot the Moon is a mediocre movie starring Albert Finney and Diane Keaton as a troubled suburban California couple in the midst of a divorce. I was watching *Shoot the Moon* on HBO, enjoying it for what it was worth—though things like movies barely made an impression on me, since I was still in the throes of ecstasy, this being the day after the walk in the snowfield—when Diane Keaton, starting to crack under the strain, does something unhealthy on screen (drinks scotch in the afternoon? takes too much Valium? I don't remember), and on the soundtrack, to illustrate the point, comes Mick Jagger singing "Nineteenth Nervous Breakdown." I had always loved the Stones, though not that particular song, but sitting on the bed, I felt my cheeks redden and my forehead begin to sweat as Mick sang on obnoxiously about the onset of multiple nervous breakdowns. Diane Keaton took her pills or drank her booze or whatever. My fists clenched.

Nineteen nervous breakdowns? Could someone have nineteen nervous breakdowns? If they could have nineteen, could they have nineteen hundred? Nineteen million? Nineteen billion? What would one look like, what would one feel like, if one suffered nineteen billion breakdowns? What would nineteen billion breakdowns feel like? Could I have nineteen billion breakdowns? Could I? Could I survive it? Stupid infernal Mick sang on, and then the song ended, and I was left with these thoughts.

For the next three months, that loop of thoughts, no more and no less than what I've written above, made me almost suicidal. It's bizarre to me. As I write these ideas down now, they cause barely a ripple of trepidation—I see them for what they are, just riffs on words and numbers having no essential meaning. But back then, the anguish! I was unable to push away the full tormenting power of those words. It barely makes sense to me now, but back then it was as if I had invented in my mind a device that measured or quantified nervous breakdowns, and the pain associated with them, and *merely by thinking about it*, I was experiencing the nervous breakdowns that killed Henry off, or for that matter Hemingway or Rothko or Virginia Woolf or anybody who's suffered mentally, at nineteen billion times the strength that they did. What would that feel like? Who could survive that? It was unspeakable, unthinkable! The crippling agony!

I turned *Shoot the Moon* off in a crippled daze and limped around the house and tried to sleep to get away from it all.

The dance in the snow of the night before seemed awfully far away.

⚬ ⚬ ⚬

At the end of January I enrolled again at Wilson for my usual group of almost randomly selected liberal arts courses. But in the middle of March, almost incapacitated by the ongoing onslaught of ideas about billions of nervous breakdowns, I walked into the registrar's office and signed the forms to withdraw from all my classes. My action still seems slightly inexplicable to me. I have never been given to making decisive and potentially troublesome choices. But amid the ongoing mental storm, one thing was clear: I had to do something; I had to get out of there. I had to escape the suffocation of ideas, or I might possibly die from them. "What the hell did you do?" said Nick, who was still getting straight As. "What are you, crazy?" I wanted to tell him yes, but didn't.

It was beginning to occur to me that the words and ideas and education and supposed sophistication that I and Henry and Nick had been inculcated with had to this point done absolutely nothing for us. Henry was in the ground, and I was constantly chased around by troubling, desperate thoughts that had become my daily reality. It occurred to me, slowly and murkily, that the intellectual hothouse environment I'd been immersed in was not helpful, in fact was highly destructive.

Having been given all the choices, I intuitively sensed I needed to go to a place where there were none. At Andover I had volunteered at a school for mildly mentally retarded children, and I had learned more in its confines than in any class at prep school. Within a week of dropping out of Wilson, I had researched job listings and found an agency that managed a group home on Atlantic Avenue. A week after that, I was hired as a "Child Care Worker" at five dollars an hour, and soon enough I was wiping drool from Luke's face. I was assigned the 3–11 p.m. shift, considered undesirable by most staff but perfect for me. I could stay out after work, driving around Cold River or hanging out with Nick, and then sleep until noon. In any case my latest choice of career seemed more interesting than washing dishes and busing tables. I regard that decision—or those decisions, to simultaneously shrug off the entirety of what my family wanted and enter a grungy, ill-paying, and seemingly dead-end job—as simply the most intelligent thing I have ever done. Even then, it was clear that this was the beginning of something, the beginning of an interior passage that would have unusual and unanticipated consequences; a route that, in ways I could never have fathomed at the time, would lead me, eventually, to people like Michael Jasny and to places like homeless shelters and to people who sat in black chairs. In that decision I escaped the confines of the comfortable and steadily upward-rising escalator of my family tradition to run scared but nonetheless *toward* something, into an unknown and unknowable forest. It was less comfortable in the woods, but at least I could go where I wanted.

My parents, on sabbatical in Italy, were not at all pleased with my decision to withdraw from a second college in as many years. My mother wrote a letter saying that I was a "wimp" and that I was not upholding my end of the family tradition, that Barbers were not the sort of people who quit and drop out and evade responsibilities and don't give it the good college try. I read the letter and seethed with a boundless anger, an anger that in my Waspish, inhibited manner, I have never imparted to my parents but that has resulted, at least partially, in the writing down of this story.

◇ ◇ ◇

Two months after buying the purple shirt (and having worn it constantly), I looked into Luke's face and saw that it was ageless. It was unlined. It was round. Luke's face was a baby's face, but in this case the baby was twenty-one years old, which was exactly my age at the time. I never got over the fact that Luke looked, at most, about two years old. Maybe he looked so young because his life wasn't as hard as I would have thought. Or maybe it was because he had been forced to lead the life of an infant, his two-and-a-half-foot-long body forever relegated to his bed or his wheelchair.

I always believed that had Luke not been severely and profoundly mentally retarded, he would have been really smart. There was something intrinsically knowing and almost aristocratic about his gaze; it was as if he were looking beyond (to what exactly?) the mundane and drab things that he found directly in front of him. There was something about his rarely changing facial expression that registered permanent horror and shock. It was as if he had been informed, at some nonexistent theoretical time before he became retarded, of his eventual fate, and that look of shock at the initial moment of comprehension had been permanently etched on his face. It was as if he knew that a random event during his mother's pregnancy had crippled his body, stunted his growth to a third of normal size, made him partially blind and deaf, made him unable to walk and barely to move, and rendered him permanently speechless and perhaps, arguably, without even the ability to think.

Luke drooled all the time. It was up to Ruby and me, his personal aides at the group home, to wipe the drool from his face and neck repeatedly throughout the afternoon and evening. Luke seemed to be similarly puzzled and horrified at his tendency to drool. Had he been capable of self-reflection, he would surely have been mortified by his drooling. Luke seemed to be fundamentally meticulous. I always thought that had his mother not contracted German measles early in her pregnancy, the intact version of Luke might have been a rather effete tax lawyer or accountant, fussy about how the figures in the reports looked on the page and forever sending them back to his secretary for corrections. "This column is not lined up quite right; could you do it again?" Or he would have been the type to remove lint from other people's suits, or point out that their ties were knotted incorrectly.

"Luke, he got it the worst," Ruby, a middle-aged Jamaican woman, said to me on my second night, as we watched a particularly violent TV movie. We'd put Luke and his five housemates (all five of them were twenty-one-year-old German measles babies) to bed for the night at 8:30 p.m. "Luke, he got it the worst. I mean all of 'em got their senses all messed up, stunted growth, no speaking, but Luke, he got them seizures. Grands mals I think they call them. If he stops breathing, or his lips turn blue, just call 911. It happens every once in a while," she said nonchalantly. Her eyes never strayed from the television, even during commercials. "But I love him; he's my little baby," she added absently. From that point on, during my entire two-and-a-half-year tenure at the group home, I could never be in Luke's presence without watching his lips for incipient blueness, or fearing that his all-knowing gaze might become suddenly ethereal or glassy. I always feared that he would die—turn blue, stop breathing, shake, do whatever it is that happens in a seizure—when I was with him. I was much more comfortable tending to Luke's compatriots at the group home, Eddie and Jaime. While they too were mentally and physically decimated by the poisons that had run through their mothers' wombs, in contrast to Luke they seemed rugged and capable.

But Luke became my favorite. Pale, weak, ethereal Luke gripped me. Perhaps it was the prospect of those terrible seizures, those seizures that might happen at any moment, which both frightened me and drew me closer to him. The fact that he could be taken from Ruby and me at any moment shook me from my characteristic lethargy and made me appreciate every aspect of his being.

The group home, which was on the outer edge of a small town about twenty miles from Cold River, had been built a few years before expressly for the purpose of housing six profoundly mentally retarded adults. All on one floor, it was a six-sided utilitarian domed structure, an angular, linear high-tech beehive. There was a wide front sidewalk, which led to two wide front doors that opened automatically. Inside there was a central day room with the television and vinyl chairs, a kitchen, and a staff office and bathroom. There was an enormously elaborate fire monitoring system. A hallway circled around the day room, and six identical bedrooms and two identical bathrooms were positioned around the circling hallway. The walls were graced with inspirational and supposedly soothing images: a whale rising from the ocean, a covered bridge in fresh snow, a dog nuzzling a cat. It was unbelievably sterile. The agency had twenty or thirty of these group homes in all; in time, working substitute shifts, I saw many of them, and each one was exactly the same.

My two other clients, Jaime and Edward, could not see or hear much either, let alone speak, but they were far less physically imperiled. Jaime was in fact rather strapping, about five feet ten with a dashing moustache that Ruby and I combed and tended for him. Jaime, who would have been Puerto Rican had he not been so impaired (somehow it was impossible to assign ethnicity to someone in that state), had thick arms and a well-developed chest. These muscles seemed to have just appeared. They could not be accounted for by any ongoing physical exercise. Jaime could walk, but that was about it. Most of the day he sat in a chair looking at the ceiling and making sounds to himself—an unaccountable clicking noise that emanated from his throat as well as occasional random hand slapping. Edward was four and a half feet tall, whippet thin. The skin all over his body was blotchy, as if acid had been spilled over him. He had thick dark curly hair and black eyes. He looked like a miniature marathon runner. Indeed he was the athlete of the group home. He acted as if he owned the place, particularly his bedroom and the bathroom, where he jumped and bounced and flailed around for as long as the staff would let him. If you didn't stop him in time, his aerobic activities had a tendency to turn ugly, and he would slap his face hard and repeatedly. Ruby said that he bit people.

Over time I began to view all three of them as ageless. They were curiously unmarked, their faces unlined and pure, their moods typically serene. I looked and felt much older than them. They looked as if they were always contemplating something, some unknown or unknowable thing. But what? They had no language. Could they think? I wondered. As the days and weeks and eventually years at the group home went by, I tried—and I know this sounds weird—I tried to be like them. That they didn't have language appealed to me. There was something brilliantly straightforward about them. Like them, I wanted to be a merely physical being. When I was with them I tried not to think, tried not to let words swim through my brain—I just was. It felt good to shut down whatever faculties I had. I was sick of my talk and joking and mindless patter. Unlike Henry, these guys were alive.

The teaching of toothbrushing was one of my primary responsibilities as a child care worker. The invisible manager of the group home (working the night shift as I did, I never saw him) left for me carefully scripted "behavior modification plans" by which I was supposed to teach the residents basic skills. I was given a workbook in which I was instructed to chronicle their progress. My teaching method, as explained minimally to me by Ruby, involved a "token economy." I would bring three pennies with me into the bathroom. At the completion of a successful task—say if Jaime cleanly uncapped the toothpaste—he would receive a penny. I would set it down loudly and ostentatiously onto the white enamel of the sink. After the completion of two more tasks (say, the bringing of the toothbrush to the mouth, and the application of brush to teeth), Jaime would receive more pennies, which again I would set down on the enamel as dramatically as I could. When three pennies were lined up on the sink (I would point to them repeatedly so there was a better chance that the clients would spot them), Jaime would be rewarded with a glass of juice.

Jaime, like Luke, seemed to possess an innate fastidiousness, and he became my star student. After four months of nightly sessions, he learned to brush his teeth more or less independently. Edward in contrast considered the introduction of the pennies as yet another anarchic activity. If by some chance he received a penny, he'd end up swiping it off the enamel, and it would ricochet off the walls. Luke, in his wheelchair, could barely grab the toothbrush with his hand. Our classes were short, and after a few minutes I would end up brushing his teeth for him.

I, who had never taught anything, who had only been taught by others, took my work seriously. Actually, I found it exhilarating to be engaged in the instruction of something real and important, unlike the absurd liberal arts courses I'd been taking. "Good man, Jaime!" I would shout. "Good man!!!" I was instructed by the invisible manager to say "good man" at any indication of "appropriate" or "goal-directed" behavior. Jaime seemed pleased, drinking his juice. He would even appear to laugh to himself, but I noticed, over time, that his laughter was never correlated with any completion of tasks or receipt of a reward. It was completely random.

But toothbrushing was not the primary interest of the residents of the group home. Masturbation was. All the clients spent great amounts of time masturbating. Masturbating—never spoken of by the staff—was the great activity, the grand passion of the house. Upon entering the day room, you might find four of six guys stroking themselves through their pajamas. (The other three clients were cared for by Ruby and so remain rather indistinct memories for me.) I was never aware that the guys ever brought themselves to orgasm. That function too, I believe, was decimated.

So it was just endless stroking. One night, toward the end of my shift, I brought a girl (not Laura, not yet) I was spending some time with for a visit to the group home. I was proud of what I was doing there and wanted to show the place off. The men had all just gone to bed, and we stepped into Jaime's room so my friend could get a quick peek at him. (Jaime slept with his light on.) Jaime had his pajamas pulled down and was stroking away. His erect penis must have been ten inches long. My friend had never seen anything quite like it. We left the room, giggling to cover our embarrassment. With deeper embarrassment, I realized later that I was jealous that I wasn't similarly endowed.

◦◦ ◦◦ ◦◦

My parents, troubled by my habit of dropping out of colleges, my odd career path, and my obvious distress (I'm sure it was more apparent than I thought it was), suggested I see a therapist. I didn't want to go, particularly, but I went.

He was a good man, and a good doctor, and we talked a lot about real things (girls and sports and school and Henry's death and the overly intellectual tendencies of me and my family, my unhelpful bent toward abstraction and so on), and I felt more normal and slightly less crazy with him, and he and his clinicians promptly made a diagnosis—obsessive compulsive disorder. It was a relief, I suppose, for there to be a name for my torment. The diagnosis, though, came as no real surprise. Years before, I think it was toward the end of high school, I was in my older brother's bedroom, looking through his bookshelf filled with his college texts. For some reason, as if drawn to it, I took out his introductory psychology textbook and turned to the chapter on "abnormal psychology." I read through the pages on anxiety disorders. The text described case studies of people who couldn't stop washing their hands, or thinking certain thoughts. It described a man who couldn't drive because he feared he would, or had, hit pedestrians. There was a passage about a mother who had recurrent thoughts about killing her baby, and a description of someone who couldn't stop repeating words from going through his head. Knowing that the descriptions applied to me, I read no more and slammed the book shut.

I saw the doctor for six months, and the simple process of talking got easier and better and I felt some mild unburdening of agony. It was helpful to talk about my family, particularly my brothers, who were both thriving. Tom was at the top of his class in medical school, and John, after graduating from Yale, was working for a top investment bank in New York. His income was approximately twenty times what mine was. I began to recognize that I had been pushed powerfully inward by my brothers' success in the exterior world. I couldn't compete with them in their careers, but I could excel in the world of morbid thought and imagination. There, nobody could keep up with me.

But all the money my parents were paying on therapy didn't seem to make much of a difference. I asked about medication, and the doctor said there was nothing appropriate. (Back then there was in fact a medication for OCD, Luvox, but it had terrible side effects. Still, I wish I'd at least been able to give it a try.) I was able to accept the diagnosis in name only and was unwilling to change much. For change to occur, I would have to really accept I had an illness, a psychiatric illness, and this was an affront I was unwilling to tolerate. Me, an illness? I didn't think so. Yes, I was eccentric and troubled and abstracted and obsessive, but I was in no way *mentally ill*. I had way too much going for me for that. So, without that fundamental acceptance on my part, all the doctor and I could do was sit there and chat pleasantly.

But something did help. The doctor referred me to a colleague, a psychologist who specialized in cognitive-behavioral therapy. I took an instant dislike to her. She was (or so I thought) humorless, severe, borderline unpleasant, and annoyingly direct, lacking in subtlety. I saw her only about ten times in the sterile office in the basement of her vinyl-sided drab house. I was typically late for the sessions and didn't feel at the time that they were doing much. And yet she has helped me more, in a certain way, than any other person in my life.

The sessions were practical and task-oriented. After the first meeting, she gave me a rubber band to put on my wrist and asked me to snap it every time I experienced an intrusive thought. Of course I ended up snapping it constantly, all day long, so much so that my wrists became inflamed. The next week she had me keep a log of my obsessions, and the week after that she asked me to rate on a scale of 1 to 10 how much distress they were causing, on an hour-by-hour basis. Mainly I wrote 8s, 9s, and 10s. These tasks had the collective impact of making me aware of how much sheer energy the OCD was taking out of me, and perhaps more important, allowed me for the first time to see the thoughts in some objective fashion, as something to be analyzed and examined, and not something at the very center of my being. In the weeks after that she trained me in breathing and relaxation exercises to employ whenever I felt overwhelmed. Finally she taught me "implosion" techniques, in which I would purposefully summon up the offending thought (still stuff about infinite nervous breakdowns) and expose myself to its full power. This flew in the face of all my previous strategies with OCD—to avoid thinking of it whenever possible. The doctor explained in her cool fashion that, over time, the act of summoning up the thoughts and flooding myself with them would show me I had control over the thoughts. She also said that as I continued with the implosion techniques, the thoughts would have less and less hold on me: I would become desensitized to their power. While this was not always the case—there were plenty of times I would bring on the thoughts and feel worse than ever and wonder why the hell I was going out of my way to think them—over time, and here I'm talking of months and years, their power over me yielded and softened.

After the last session, I said a perfunctory good-bye and thanks to the woman, not yet realizing that I would employ her techniques daily for the rest of my life.

In time—working at the group home, hanging out with Nick and Bill and Laura, reading constantly, starting to exercise again, slowly adopting the cognitive-behavioral techniques—things softened somewhat. I saw there were things to live for, and I no longer exclusively inhabited a tragic world.

❖ ❖ ❖

Eddie was crazy in the shower. He would throw the soap away and then jump like a pogo stick sixty times in the air. As I attempted to dry him, he would wheel away and touch his toes thirty times over, making excited chortling sounds as he did so. At the height of his energy, he would cackle with glee. Or he would throw down the toothbrush and smack the tile walls with his open hand as many times as he could before I pulled him away.

Trying to restrain Eddie was an equally aerobic activity. As I was never, amazingly, trained in any kind of restraint techniques, I simply made it up as I went along. I would think of an imaginary box around him and try to keep him within its confines. In time, I learned from Ruby that the principal reason I had been hired was to control Eddie. "I was real relieved when you showed up," Ruby said. "I couldn't take him no more."

One night, maybe six months after I started, Eddie was particularly manic. "Give him a shower," Ruby said. "Do your best to control him." I had learned that the one thing you couldn't do in tending Eddie was pause to think—you needed simply to move and respond to his movements. I made the mistake that night in the bathroom, as he was flailing away energetically, of hesitating for a moment while planning my next move. In a flash, Eddie grabbed my arm, positioned my hand in his mouth, and sank his teeth into me.

"Goddamnit!" I shouted. I pushed him aside and wrangled my hand away. I looked down to see that the fleshy part of my right thumb had two sets of perfectly matched indentations oozing blood. Eddie had extracted no pieces of flesh, but had bitten down deeply into me. I pushed him again, hard. I went to the sink and let the cold water flow over the wound for minutes. It started to throb. A long trail of blood eddied down the drain. Eddie, as if in penance, went to the corner and starting slapping his face. I let him slap away.

After controlling the bleeding, I wrapped my hand in a towel and went to see Ruby. "You better go to the ER," she said sharply.

Ruby gave me directions to a twenty-four-hour medical center. My thumb wrapped up, I drove through the soft summer rain, down through the woods and the hills to the small highway that led into the flat suburban world of the large city near Cold River. I must have driven through twenty stoplights, past fifteen minimalls and six supermarkets, until I arrived at the "medical center," a little office situated in a flimsy cube of a building that looked like it had been built in about two weeks. I immediately saw the doctor, a young Pakistani or Indian man. I explained about the bite, and within thirty seconds he administered a perfectly aimed tetanus shot into my arm. It was painless. I then filled out the paperwork, smiling genially. He couldn't have been more pleasant or competent.

Maybe it was a delayed reaction to having been bitten, or maybe it was just a late surge of adrenaline, but out of nowhere I felt a sudden and completely unjustified rage toward the doctor. Actually, that's not right, I'm being too understated: I wanted to kill him. Somehow the frustrations of the night, or perhaps the frustrations of the last few years, came out and found their target in him. Perhaps if I hadn't grown up so suburban and comfortable, if I hadn't had class and decorum so delicately but brutally foisted on me, if I hadn't been railroaded (as I felt about it in that moment) by the last three years of bad thoughts, I might be the doctor here, I thought. I hated him and I hated Henry and I hated that Henry died and I hated that I couldn't control Eddie and I hated that I couldn't finish college and that I was miserable and inept. I hated, mainly, myself. It wasn't like before, in Harvard Yard, when I recoiled against the intrusion of murderous thoughts. This time I just wanted to fucking kill the guy, to jump on him and beat him up. I wanted a fight. I loomed over him; I wanted to show my strength and rage. But no one, least of all the doctor, could have detected what I was thinking. I shook his hand politely and thanked him very much for his assistance.

In the days after the bite, I examined my purplish thumb with satisfaction and marveled at the perfectly symmetrical indentations created by Eddie's teeth. I proudly showed my wound to my parents, and anybody who would look at it. Finally I had something to show for my tribulations.

◦ ◦ ◦

My brother Tom, then a medical student, called me and said there was a rerelease of a Hitchcock film from the 1950s, *Rear Window*. I recall meeting Tom at the theater in my typical obsessive funk—the usual violent, angry ideas. The movie had been Tom's idea, and I had no particular expectations for it.

I sat in the dark theater and spent the next two hours in another world. *Rear Window* was so mesmerizing that I simply forgot the painful oblivion in which I had been living. I moved through it and beyond it, and became solely an instrument able to experience the film. I was captivated and removed. No longer was I near Cold River . . . no longer was I in the misery of my own head . . . but somewhere else, a place exquisitely artistic and deeply expressive.

Leaving the theater, I felt exhilarated, renewed. I experienced the kind of endorphin infusion one feels after exercising. My body felt good again, almost glowing. I remember standing with Tom in the parking lot afterward, feeling the cool air, looking at the highway and the industrial plants around us. The dull landscape had been transformed. The world glistened again.

◦ ◦ ◦

In William Styron's confession of his bout with madness, *Darkness Visible*, he describes being rescued from the throes of suicide upon hearing, almost by chance, Brahms's *Alto Rhapsody*. The extraordinary lush and beautiful sounds transported him, suddenly, into a revelation of the pleasures that still existed for him in the world. How could he take his life, Styron thought, when creations like the *Alto Rhapsody*, and the associated pleasures of home and work and family, exist in the world? It wasn't possible.

But *Rear Window* was not beautiful in that way. It was neither exalted nor dignified. Indeed, it was precisely because its themes (sex, murder, violence, obsession, compulsion) were crass, precisely because it took on awfulness and sordidness and guilt, that it was so powerful. That something of such sheer exhilarating excellence had been created from the same emotions that had surely contributed to Henry's decision to die made the notion of my own self-destruction, in a moment, absurd. The experience of seeing *Rear Window* effectively repelled the notion of suicide. Those thoughts were drawn off me like water flowing off well-oiled leather. With creations like *Rear Window* in the world, suicide seemed just silly. Hitchcock had recognized the horror of the world, and then transformed that horror into something entirely different.

While I had always held vague ambitions about writing, it was art like *Rear Window* that made me feel pressingly for the first time that I really needed to put Henry's story, and other stories, down on paper. And there were other disparate influences around that same time. I remember being startled by the apocalyptic but somehow redemptive vision of the world expressed in Walker Percy's novel *Love in the Ruins*, and also deeply affected, I'm almost embarrassed to admit, by a book of interviews done with John Lennon just before his death. I still frequented the Wilson library, and in the stacks at two in the morning, after my shift, I came across a book of interviews with Lennon and stayed up all night reading it. ("What's the matter with you," Ruby said the next day. "Didn't get no sleep?") Lennon's words, as he acknowledged his own passage of despair (he was suicidal even at the height of his success with the Beatles), were marvelously naked and real. They gave me hope. For months I carried around that book of interviews, my own secular bible.

But all these years later, *Rear Window* is what stands out. It seems odd that a film should have helped rescue me. Despite the black thoughts, at the time I had my brothers, my parents, a job I liked . . . but it was *Rear Window* that gave me something to live for. I was cleansed and renewed by Hitchcock's ability to murder and create.

꘡ ꘡ ꘡

I still saw friends from Wilson, most notably Bill and Laura. Bill and I continued to share our enthusiasms for Eugene O'Neill and Miles Davis and Prince and Raymond Carver, and we would go on long late-night treks around Cold River talking about them, and our own artistic aspirations. Laura would join us sometimes, and we would go out for pizza or to a movie and back for coffee at their apartment. There were at times obvious tensions between Bill and Laura, mainly because he was focused on his writing and not on her. Sometimes Bill wasn't around, and Laura and I would go out driving around Cold River, and I would show her the local haunts that Henry and Nick and I used to frequent. We would go to Dunkin' Donuts and the Salvation Army and Goodwill, and she would buy odd artifacts that were Henry-like in their eccentricity, and we would laugh and joke and she would make me feel better. We spent more and more time together, and I thought more and more often about her petite curves and felt more in the world when I was with her. Bill and she were still together, though, and I was not going to make any advance while that was still the case. That was my excuse, anyway: the truth was I didn't really know how to make a move.

I so liked the group home that I took a weekend job at another one. This facility was entirely different, located on a suburban street, in a red 1950s three-story handsome colonial house. The men at this group home, too, were quite different; they were, as they say in the trade, much higher functioning. What this principally meant was that they could speak. They could speak! After a year and a half with Eddie and Luke, this was a relief. Of course the mens' language was disjointed and hesitant, but for me it was like water flowing again. This mirrored my own sense of progress; after a year, I felt ready to reenter the world of language and expression.

Four of the six men were retarded as a result of anoxia, a lack of oxygen in the first few minutes after birth. Those who had been deprived of oxygen the longest were the most impaired. Unlike the residents of the first group home, who were poisoned in utero, these men's bodies and brains at least came into the world more or less intact; the insult occurred upon arrival. The other two residents, Seth and Keith, had different sources of retardation and, not coincidentally, were the outcasts. Keith suffered from the chromosomal abnormality that causes Down syndrome, and Seth probably wasn't technically mentally retarded at all. His IQ was probably somewhere around 80, whereas 70 or below is mentally retarded. Seth, a misfit among misfits, was there simply because he had no other place to go.

As if united by their shared trauma, the four men who had suffered from anoxia occupied the social center of the group home and created its social norms. The four of them had lived together for ten years, and they traveled almost as a unit. I began to think of them as the Gang of Four. Only they could understand each other's own broken and idiosyncratic language and gestures; the staff and I would often have to ask one resident what the other was trying to convey.

The overriding philosophy of the place was, purportedly, to normalize the men. The idea was to "mainstream" them, to erode the institutional lethargy resulting from the decades that most of them had spent essentially imprisoned in state facilities. In that normal house in a normal neighborhood, the staff and I were supposed to introduce the clients to the activities of everyday life: cleaning, cooking, budgeting, shopping, socializing, attending church, going out to movies and restaurants. Monday to Friday, all six residents participated in a sheltered workshop, where they made paper flowers. The desire to expose them to the world was noble, I'm sure, but often the men, unable to complete simple tasks like unloading the dishwasher, would get frustrated and sullen and walk away to be silent in their rooms.

The men were extraordinarily attuned to pop culture. All of us spent great amounts of time watching MTV. Their tastes uniformly gravitated toward whatever was at the very center of the culture at that moment. They all loved Reagan, Rambo, Madonna, Michael Jackson—whoever was supposed to be "normal." (Although all of those icons of the early 1980s seem deeply twisted to me now.) But if Madonna dropped in the charts, or was considered "too weird" (as when she later became more sexually explicit), she was replaced in their hierarchy by the next pop star. The men could have been employed as social barometers, exactly calibrated to sense what was most normal or popular. I used to think that the guys could have been used as highly accurate polling devices for national elections.

I saw that there was a great divide between those clients who knew they were retarded and those who didn't. Those who were unaware, it seemed to me, were blissfully unaware. They pursued things with an enviable simplicity and ease. I am convinced that they were far, far happier than people "on the outside," as they always referred to the rest of the world. Those who were aware of their disability, though, were somehow blighted. They still had a joy and simplicity but also a lingering sadness about their differentness that followed them everywhere. They became self-conscious in public, quiet and downcast. They would uncharacteristically stutter at the cash register, or ask the staff to order food for them at restaurants when they knew how to do it themselves. They lost the boisterousness and flow that we enjoyed when we were all together in the house.

    ❖ ❖ ❖

Meanwhile Nick had graduated from the college at the top of his class. But in his senior year he seemed to have lost his momentum and drive for achievement. I can't think of anything he did differently (he still excelled at school); it was more of a look in his eyes. Whereas once he had only read about "the absurd," in Camus and other existentialist writers, he now embraced irreverence bordering on despair in a way that only Henry and I had previously. Nick, I see now, took Henry's death much harder than I did. I had always suspected Nick of being a far more sentimental person than I was—I obsess and ruminate, which is a very different thing from feeling—and that heavy, dull look in his eyes that never disappeared acted to confirm that belief.

With no particular job prospects, at least until the fall when he planned to work on his high school teaching certificate (which in itself seemed a long way from his earlier ambition to become a famous writer), Nick joined me at the second group home. I was thrilled that he and I were back together. It was as if we were back in college or high school. The group home seemed an odd place to reunite, but somehow appropriate too, very much in the Henry Court absurdist tradition, we agreed. Nick and I prevailed on the home's invisible manager, whom we rarely saw, to arrange the schedule so we could work weekends together. In our own fashion, we tried to "normalize" the men. This meant we did with them what we used to do with Henry, the usual nonactivities, like walking in circles around the neighborhood and introducing them to the pleasures of aimless driving in the group home's Ford Country Squire station wagon. We'd all pile in the ridiculously large vehicle and get lost in the remote towns around Cold River. The six men effectively replaced Henry as our lost driving companion.

Most of the residents were from Catholic families, and Nick and I were charged with taking them to Mass on Sundays. The men sat more or less quietly during the ceremony, fidgeting more as it got closer to the Eucharist. The Eucharist was, for all of them, the highlight of the ceremony. Some of them knew some of the recitations ("And forever and ever, amen"; "This is the word of the Lord"; "For yours is the power and the glory"; "Peace be with you"), and the more self-conscious guys carefully monitored other congregants for cues to when to stand, sit, and pray. When the time came for the Eucharist, they rose as a group and filed in unison toward the altar, receiving the wafer and grape juice (not wine) in order. The more aware ones adopted an appropriately somber look, which was the same exact look that most of the parishioners had, in tune with the gravity of receiving the body and blood of Christ. Depending on his relationship with the creator on any given Sunday, Nick remained in his seat or went to receive the sacrament with the guys. Most times he sat and watched. I, the non-Catholic, always stayed where I was, preferring to observe. The churchgoers always looked self-conscious around the men, either annoyed or conspicuously moved. After the ceremony we usually went to a country store and bought muffins. We'd all eat them sitting in the station wagon. Bob, the largest of the men, munched the muffins appreciatively. "This is really good," he'd say. "It's not like that tiny little wafer they gave us back at the church!"

Seth served equally as the group's leader and their outcast. Seth looked exactly like Jerry Lewis in his early movies, plus twenty pounds. He had the interesting quality of being exceptionally good-natured and nervous, both at the same time. In the absence of the staff, the men followed his direction but then resented him for it. Seth didn't fit in anywhere. He had been in the Navy, unbelievably, for about two months, but he had a nervous breakdown there and had spent most of the rest of his twenties and thirties in nursing homes, even though he didn't have any pressing medical problems. He befriended the more alert patients and acted as a sort of staff adjunct, running errands. He was needy and anxious, and his family didn't want him living with them.

Seth was Jewish, and after months of going to Catholic churches, he wanted desperately to go to temple. "Equal rights, Charlie," he would say to me, laughing. To assuage him, I accompanied him to the synagogue in Cold River. There are few Jewish families in Cold River, and the synagogue is small and intimate. The bubble of intimacy was immediately broken when Seth and I entered the lobby of the temple. The congregants turned around and stared at us, unsure of who we were exactly, and why we were there. Seth and I were an odd couple, for sure—the tall awkward Wasp and the young manic Jerry Lewis.

Seth had a habit of checking the change slots of all the pay phones he came across for coins. In fact this was his primary daily activity. In his daylong outings in search of cheap cigarettes and soda, he checked every pay phone in his path, and would return exultant to the group home if he happened to find a dime or quarter. In the lobby of the synagogue, he spied a pay phone. I attempted to stop him but it was too late. He headed directly for it through the crowd of people greeting each other and, arriving at the phone, fished ostentatiously for change. There was none. He headed back to me, through the now-staring crowd.

"Oh, Charlie," Seth said, "I'm sorry I did that, people might think I'm JEWISH or something." He laughed uproariously.

There was complete silence in the lobby. First the mood was one of shock, but then it turned, I think, into anger. The group stared harshly at me, sensing that I was the party responsible for this unwelcome visit, and then drew collectively back, heading up the stairs for the service. I wanted to bolt, but Seth was entirely oblivious to any sense of embarrassment. He didn't understand why the crowd hadn't appreciated his rather witty humor. He bounded up the stairs after the rest of the congregants, excited to be finally attending a service in his own faith.

Once in the temple itself, I regained my composure enough to direct Seth, by grabbing his arm, to sit in a row discretely near the back. On our way to be seated, an usher handed us yarmulkes. Seth and I took them and placed them on our heads.

"This is great," Seth said loudly. "It'll cover my bald spot! And yours too, Charlie! Although yours is just thinning!"

"Shut up, Seth," I said. If any of the people in attendance had forgotten us, they now looked back at us from the rows ahead with angry, daggerlike stares. My face reddened and I started to sweat.

The service began, and I attempted to calm myself listening to the chants and rituals. This seemed to work well enough until I leaned back and my yarmulke dropped off my head and directly into the lap of the man in the row behind me. He tapped me on the shoulder and handed it back to me. After that, I just waited for the service to end and hoped that Seth wouldn't do or say anything more.

"Thanks, Charlie, thanks a lot! I really appreciate it," Seth said as we descended the staircase after the service. "I really appreciate it, because I am Jewish, you know."

I nodded, escorting him as swiftly as I could past the pay phone.

⋯ ⋯ ⋯

Keith, with Down syndrome, laughed uproariously at anything he came upon. He laughed at a shoe; he laughed at a cup of coffee; he laughed at a lampshade. Nick and I would typically be puzzled at the source of Keith's humor, but more often than not, his sheer lunacy would compel us to end up laughing with him. The others would roll their eyes at his "inappropriate" belly laughs, especially if they occurred in public, and when he found something particularly hilarious, they would move away from him, as if in a unit. It seems to me now, looking back on it, that Keith remains one of the most preternaturally happy people I have ever known.

On warmer days, Keith would wait for me to show up for work on the back patio in a tank top and shorts, sitting on a lawn chair, drinking a soda and enjoying suburbia. I would pull up in my vw Rabbit, newly and proudly purchased with wages, turn down the loud music I was playing, and jump out of the car in a hurry.

"How ya, how ya, how ya doing, Chaaaaalie!" Keith would say, and burst out, of course, laughing. He would repeat his greeting, laugh so hard that he would almost fall out of the chair. He would laugh so hard he would disturb the neighbors.

After this greeting ritual went on all summer, Keith began asking me, and then imploring me, to let him get in the car and come for a drive. "No, I can't do that," I'd say, thinking that our invisible manager wouldn't be happy if we got into an accident. "No, no," I'd say to

Keith. He'd pretend to get very angry, stop speaking to me for ten minutes, and occasionally kick his yard chair so that it tipped over on the ground. Then he would smile at me again impishly, and all was forgiven.

I finally broke down one day and told him to get in the car right after I arrived for work. His eyes widened, and he moved his round body out of the chair faster than I thought he was capable of and ran to the Volkswagen. The bucket seat barely contained him. He was so excited that he was almost wheezing. I put on his seat belt, which was another tight fit, and pulled out of the driveway. Within minutes we were out in the countryside around Cold River, driving up and down the wooded hills, listening to Bob Dylan whine away at his beautiful songs.

"Play Bob Dylan loud, Chaaalie!" Keith shouted.

I turned the volume up a bit.

Clearly this wasn't good enough. "Play Bob Dylan louder, Chaalie!" he shouted again, almost irritably, had he been capable of irritability.

I turned the volume up again. This satisfied him for the moment, but not for long. "Play Bob Dylan LOUDER, Chaaaaaaalliie!!!"

"Okay." I turned the cassette player up as high as it could go, so that Bob Dylan's nasal twang, sometimes difficult to take at muted volume, became overwhelming. Bob sang, "MAN THINKS IF HE RULES THE WORLD, HE CAN DO WHATEVER HE PLEASE," to which Keith sang, "MAN THINKS IF HE RULES THE WORLD, HE CAN DO WHATEVER HE PLEASE!!!" and then added, "nnnuech, nnnuech, nnneuch!!!" It went on, just like that, Bob and Keith, with some Three Stooges added in for the chorus, for some time.

At a certain moment, as Keith and I rolled up and down through the woods, it dawned on me that I had arrived at a certain consequential point in my education. This, it seemed, was learning and true experience; this was original, and real, and alive; and this was far, far more interesting than anything I could have learned in the confines of Harvard Yard. As Keith sang, I felt momentarily exhilarated and realized, with no small satisfaction, that I had not let my schooling interfere with my education.

◦ ◦ ◦

Bill and Laura broke up. Bill went off for the summer to teach artsy high school students at the Wellesley summer school, and when he came back he broke things off with her, or she broke things off with him, I'm not sure which, and two days later Laura and I were lying next to each other in a field behind St. Joe's, my old high school. We didn't have much time to spend together, though, because in two weeks she was moving to a village in upstate New York to curate the estate of a famous photographer on a National Endowment for the Arts fellowship. We were inseparable those two weeks, going swimming, watching videos (Woody Allen's *Manhattan* was the first movie we watched), and simply hanging out at the palatial house where she was housesitting. We kissed and made out, and I helped her pack up and move, and we resolved to see each other every weekend: I would drive to her upstate town, and she would come visit me in Cambridge.

Yes, after two years at group homes I had decided to return to Harvard. I felt up to it. The obsessive thoughts had melted some. I was ready for language and thought again. I had healed in those two years, as the result of a combination of cognitive-behavioral therapy, my education at the group home, and now Laura. I was ready to return to Harvard University, which I now regarded with a certain healthy vigor as simply a very large group home of its own, complete with its own token economy.

Everybody was thrilled about it. My parents told all their friends the news. If Charlie was at Harvard, the unspoken thought was, he had to be all right. The official, superficial, and exterior version of reality was all that counted. The weird affliction that had taken over their son, this extended period in the wilderness, this strange interior plague was now pronounced over. Nick, though, stayed on at the group home and works there to this day.

.<o .<o .<o

Just before my return to Cambridge, I watched Mrs. Court order a steady stream of scotches at a restaurant in the middle of Kansas, and wondered why they seemingly had no impact on her. I had heard stories of her alcoholic adventures, stories about her showing up at her classes on the literature of World War I drunk, of disappearing in the department offices for a day or two at a time and then being discovered passed out in one of her colleague's offices. I had heard that she had separated from William, and that he had moved out of the condo to his own apartment on campus. But when I saw her, two and a half years after Henry's funeral, she looked to me just the same: buoyant, expressive, inappropriately effusive. The only difference I could see was that five scotches seemed to have no appreciable effect on her, and I figured it was because this was just part of her daily regimen.

Mrs. Court and I sat across from each other at a table at the Sirloin Stockade in a small town in Kansas. What exactly she was doing in Kansas I never really knew. She explained to me that she was doing "research"—something having to do with Dwight Eisenhower. Indeed, Eisenhower had grown up in the town (he was my grandparents' high school classmate), and his presidential library is there. But what this scholar of Virginia Woolf and Rupert Brooke and Wilfred Owen was doing with Eisenhower I couldn't imagine. The only commonality I could think of was war, either internal or external. I was in Kansas because my grandmother, who had lived in this Kansas town most of her life, had become senile, and my parents and I were moving her to a nursing home. Her house was being sold, and we were clearing out the detritus of her life. I don't know how many *National Geographic* and *Good Housekeeping* magazines, cans of pickles, Christmas cards, and thousands of old letters we threw out that week. We also found the notes describing the story of William and Joseph Barber swimming ashore after the shipwreck. I wondered if Mrs. Court's appearance in remote Kansas, at the same time that my parents and I were there, was just coincidence. I even wondered if perhaps she was in Kansas to see me.

It was I who spoke of Henry first. But once I did, it opened for her a floodgate of memory and passion. Mrs. Court began to speak of a person I no longer knew. The person she spoke of was gentle, noble, stable, and kind. Henry was all of those things, but not very often. At one point, I think I remember, she spoke of her departed angel, he of the pale skin and delicate, handsome face.

At the end of our meal, Mrs. Court spoke drunkenly and with particular enthusiasm about a scholarship she had endowed in Henry's honor, the "Henry S. Court Scholarship" for the highest-scoring boy on the entrance exam to St. Joe's. I cringed. If there was one place that

Henry wouldn't want his family's hard-earned money going to, it was to the nerds at St. Joe's he'd spent four years making fun of.

We walked to the parking lot, kissed good-bye, and got into our rental cars. I had to get up early; we had a lot of moving to do in the morning.

That was the last time I saw her.

six

Prozac and Diet Coke

Laura and I did see each other every weekend that fall, making long treks along the Massachusetts Turnpike. In Cambridge, we would stay in my dorm room, go to the bookstores, and see old movies at the Brattle Square theater. In her upstate New York town, we'd go for long walks, sleep in, have brunch at the village diner. She'd show me the photographs she was working on. We would write postcards to each other during the week, funny notes to each other on the weekends. I was not a virgin but I was inexperienced, and Laura provided a kind of erotic initiation for me, creating sensations and feelings and excitement that I didn't know existed. With her, I felt like I no longer carried the sole burden of the things that bothered me. I was enveloped by her and in her, in a deep hard intimacy that kept bad things at bay. Laura gave me things that Henry never had. In time I told Laura all about the OCD, and she simply held me, patting my head, and thought nothing less of me. She has never been the least bit judgmental about it, simply regarding it as something to be dealt with.

Harvard, though, was another matter. The less said about it, the better. Not that it was so bad or awful—nothing, thankfully, as debilitating as my freshman-year experience, when I wanted to murder my fellow undergraduates. It was just that I felt, as sophomore year turned to junior year turned to senior year, an increasing sense of dread. The positive momentum created by my experience at the group home gradually receded and was replaced by more and more troublesome thoughts. Perhaps I was not yet ready for a return to a competitive environment—the stress of getting back in the game—but when I think about Harvard, I am acutely aware that it was not, never was, my territory. It was my father's and my brother's university. They had preceded me there and had claimed it for their own.

A few years later, when I went to graduate school at the School of the Arts at Columbia, it was like entering fresh, uncharted territory. My experience there was infinitely better, probably having nothing to do with objective matters but having everything to do with the fact that finally I was making my own way. I felt like I had broken out of those familial paths that had been preestablished for me, as well as the oppressive confines of my personal history in Cold River.

I will always love Columbia University. This no doubt has something to do with its educational excellence, but principally it's because it was at Columbia that I decided, finally and resolutely, to do something about the OCD.

⊷ ⊷ ⊷

The subway station at 160th Street in Manhattan is so ugly that it's almost beautiful. It's buried six floors below ground, deep into the recesses of the island, and it's separated from the surface of the city and the clarity of daylight by a single barely functioning elevator. Actually, there is a bank of four elevators, but only one of them ever seems to be working. In the summer months it is sweltering in the tunnels of the station, and the single elevator is cooled by means of a small fan that stands next to the stool on which the elevator operator sits, sweating and listening all day long to 1960s soul music on a boombox. The smell that overwhelms the entire station is a powerful, curious mixture of ammonia and urine. The ammonia is intended to erase the smell of urine, but the urine always seems to get the upper hand. The air in the station is for some reason always foggy, not from any ostensible smoke or exhaust or combustion of urine and ammonia, but from something, I think, relating to the precise depth of the station below the surface of Manhattan and the sheer grayness of everything down there. Everything is gray, or black: the trains, the platforms, the tunnels as they fade off in the distance, and the discarded chewing gum of generations of travelers, creating a pockmarked environment of endless black spots on the walkways.

By means of the slow, single elevator, I rose out of the earth to 168th street, which is equally chaotic and jumbled. The neighborhood itself seems like some displaced part of the Caribbean, given the huge number of Dominicans who have settled there. I headed west along 168th Street until I found my destination: 722 West 168th Street. It was another beautiful-ugly affair, a dour sand-colored brick building emitting a sense of industry and purpose. Decades of science, the building seemed to say, have been conducted in these halls.

I walked into the New York State Psychiatric Institute, stopping at the front desk to tell the attendant whom I was there to see. I went into the elevator and then I went back down again, back into the earth seven floors below Manhattan. I walked through a dingy but clean hall, past one dark-brown oak door after another, all with the names of doctors on them. The doorway to the stairwell was open. I noticed that thick wire mesh was installed between the gaps in the flights of stairs, presumably to stop anybody's fatal fall down the stairwell. I found the dark oak door with the name on it I was looking for, and knocked.

The psychiatrist, Dr. Porter, was well-built, clear-eyed, his thinning hair slicked back. I guessed he was just a few years older than I was. Indeed his diplomas indicated that he'd gone to the same universities I had, a few years before me. I sat down in his cramped office, took a deep breath, and told him reluctantly, hesitatingly at first, and then slightly more fluently as I went along, about repetitive words, fears of hurting people, worries about being connected to vast destructiveness. This was far, far different from my first exposure to a psychologist—here I told the complete truth about what bothered me, and this time I was there not at my parents' suggestion but on my own initiative. Dr. Porter listened quietly but empathetically to what I had to say, asking me the rare question. He made me feel comfortable. Things felt slightly clearer by the time I left.

After two sessions, Dr. Porter prescribed a medication called Prozac. I had recently heard of Prozac because of the sensational press it had received. It had just been on the cover of *Newsweek* and was being characterized alternatively as a wonder drug and as a toxic substance that put vulnerable people over the edge; there had been many reports of people committing suicide shortly after taking the medication. Dr. Porter, in his eminently sane manner, dismissed both characterizations of Prozac as overblown, and said that I should limit my concerns to the known side effects, which included weight loss or gain, increased or decreased libido, and racing thoughts. Of course, given my past experiences of homicidal and suicidal thoughts, I was worried about the headlines. But Dr. Porter's confident pronouncements reassured me, and I went forward without too much trepidation. And in all of this, I felt like I didn't have much choice but to give Prozac a try. I was ready.

~∽ ~∽ ~∽

It's hard to say what precipitated my voluntary visit to a psychiatrist. At Columbia I had on a daily, if not hourly, basis continued to experience "negative thinking," the term I had learned to give to the obsessive thoughts. My mind was still filled with the endless cartoon of awful things—the murders I feared I had committed, the unending sequences of words and numbers, the awful destructiveness I felt responsible for, etc. At the same time I had become expert at managing or—a better word—tolerating them, and pretending that they didn't exist. I had also learned to act as if there were nothing wrong. I had become a brilliant actor. I taught myself to exude a breezy, almost happy-go-lucky quality. I had been able to function. But things had occurred right before my visit to Dr. Porter that made me lose my balance.

Laura and I were having our first difficulties. Part of the reason was geographical—as I had moved to New York City from Cambridge, she had moved from upstate New York to Cambridge, to do a master's degree at the Harvard School of Education. She was having doubts about a career strictly in photography and was pursuing a master's degree in counseling, with the ultimate goal of getting a PhD in clinical psychology. It was crazy that she moved to while I moved away from Cambridge, and the weekend traveling had become difficult. I had grown remote and aloof, and some of our natural differences (Laura's directness and pragmatism versus my abstractness and impracticality) had deepened and turned into sources of conflict. And I am not good with conflict: I try to avoid it all costs, usually making things much worse in the process. Laura was getting increasingly exasperated with me as I lied about unpleasant things—from not telling her about the accruing fines on a parking ticket to telling her I was doing great when I actually felt deeply disturbed. We agreed to separate. She started seeing someone else, and even though that relationship was not serious, it made me feel terrible and angry.

The weekend before, I had gone to Cold River to see Nick and my parents. I hadn't felt "normal" for a few weeks. No doubt this was a direct result of the separation from Laura, although I didn't necessarily see it that way at the time. Bad thoughts plagued me like never before. Specifically—and this is deeply embarrassing for me to write about—I had further developed my earlier phobia about getting erections in public. My puritanical self-damning side had always made me fundamentally feel—in spite of my better and freer and more rational self—that overt sexuality must be associated with violence and aggression. Some part of my being believed, as I wrote earlier, that getting an erection in public was so vastly inappropriate that something awful and harmful would necessarily have to result from it. Over time I figured out, in a pathological way, a mechanism about how this could be so. My mad thinking, developed over many months, was this: Over the years—and it was years, because the phobia that developed in early adolescence had always stayed with me, although for the vast majority of the time in the back of my mind—I saw how occasionally incapacitating my fear of erections could be. It could be deeply disturbing and prevent me from functioning in the way I wanted to; it might cause me anxiety during an interview, or distract me for a few moments or minutes while I was driving. But it was not so much that it affected my functioning, it was the idea that it could. I "reasoned" that if the phobia about erections could incapacitate me so much, it could bother other people as well, and it could be linked to tragic events. So when I read about a plane crash that killed 112 people in Japan, I would think that maybe it happened because the pilot, when making his fatal error, had been distracted by concerns about his own inappropriate erections, and furthermore that the pilot had been "infected" by me—that is, he had seen me, at some airport or somewhere, with an obvious erection and had himself gotten obsessed with the same problem.

Don't worry. It makes no sense, as is the case with virtually all obsessive-compulsive pathology. I understood that these theories were crazy, insane, not worth even thinking about it, but I could never ever dismiss them from my mind. (In France, OCD is called, appropriately, the "doubting disease.") In the madness of my disturbance, I didn't go through the nonsensical steps; I just believed that I was linked to a chain of events that could have contributed to the deaths of a lot of people. This was intolerable to me. It made me despair and feel truly suicidal in a way I never had before. I felt disturbed, angry, hostile; my fists clenched as they had been in Harvard Yard. In my classes at graduate school, I found myself once again unable to think, to wrap my brain around words. I felt that I would never be able to think a natural, organic, healthy thought again. In those last few weeks, I felt truly ill, mentally sick, sick in the head.

In the subway on Friday afternoon on my way to the train at Grand Central, it was hot, crowded. I hadn't eaten all day—an indigent graduate student, I had run out of money, and one of the reasons for my trip to Cold River was to request, in humiliation, some cash from my parents to get me through the semester. Jostled by other passengers, I felt aggressive, overwhelmed, crazy. I saw the subway car and the station and New York and America and the world and the universe and God and everything else before me collapse into nothing, and I felt part of that, even a cause of it. I was in the very midst of a great destructiveness, a huge mental storm.

The next day I visited Nick. I had not seen him in a couple of years, but everything was still the same between us, which was wonderfully reassuring under the circumstances. We played chess on his porch in the afternoon sun. I'm not much of a chess player, and keeping up with Nick required a good deal of concentration, but in my state, I knew I didn't have a chance. A few moves into the game, I got caught in a loop of obsessive thinking and was unable to make a move. I couldn't think! I sat there for two minutes, doing nothing. Blindly, I just moved any old piece. Whatever move I made, it made no sense.

"What are you doing?" Nick said, promptly checkmating me.

I must have looked visibly disturbed. "Are you okay?" Nick said.

"I think I have to go home," I said, barely able to get the words out. On the way home I drove unsteadily and feared that I would hit cars and pedestrians. The whole way home that loop of thought (I don't even remember exactly what it was) stayed monolithically in my brain. I stumbled into the house and tried to sleep. My entire body hurt, as if whipped by a rubber hose. When I returned to Columbia on Monday, I made a call to the student mental health center. After a few sessions with a sympathetic therapist, she recognized what she saw and referred me to Dr. Porter and "pharmacological treatment" at the hospital.

⋯ ⋯ ⋯

I was excited to fill Dr. Porter's prescription for Prozac. Of course, many people are reluctant to take medications, particularly psychiatric ones, but I wasn't. I had been waiting for this for years. It felt somehow personally historic as I dropped off the prescription at a small pharmacy on Amsterdam Avenue. I was told to wait half an hour. I got a cup of coffee and sat in the sculpture garden of St. John the Divine Cathedral and watched the late afternoon stream of New Yorkers go by. I tried not to think my negative thoughts. I drank my coffee with a sense of anticipation.

When I returned to the pharmacy to pick up the order, I was floored at the price: $140, more than $2 a pill. This was money I didn't have, but somehow I would find it, even if it meant not eating. I put the bill on a credit card, the first of many such charges. By the time I finished graduate school I owed many thousands of dollars to Visa, all for Prozac. I opened the bottle and looked down at the sixty oblong pills, half-green and half-white. It was a rather drab green. I was disappointed in the colors; I was hoping for something that radiated a palpable sense of promise, such as vibrant yellow, orange, or purple. These color schemes, I notice, have been adopted by later generations of antidepressants.

I bought a Diet Coke and swallowed the pills at once. I wondered at the marvels of late twentieth-century science, which could produce two such entirely synthetic substances. If Prozac was as good a product as Diet Coke, I thought, I was in luck.

Dr. Porter had explained in his intelligent, soothing tones that it took a long time for the drug to be absorbed into the body—after three weeks, only half of the fluoxetine (the scientific name for Prozac) would be fully absorbed. In other words, if the medication did have an effect, I wouldn't know for almost a month. I drank my Prozac and Diet Coke. It tasted good. I felt a feeling of anticipation and potential newness.

Now all I had to do was wait.

⋆ ⋆ ⋆

Exactly twenty-one days later (I was keeping track of the days), I stood on the corner of Prince Street and Broadway in lower Manhattan. It was seven o'clock in the evening, early summer, and the taxis and buildings made dark angular shadows as the sun set across the Hudson over New Jersey. I had just finished work for the day at my summer job, as an assistant editor at a medical film company located in a Soho loft a block away. I stood at the corner, waiting for the "Walk" sign to glow so I could cross the street. Yellow taxis sailed past me at fifty miles an hour. The energy of New York was swift and real.

It was in that one moment (I swear it happened in a moment), as I waited for the light to change, that I felt the chemicals percolate into my brain. It was like a warm, gurgling running feeling in my head, like a little tap of water had been turned on somewhere. The fluoxetine had arrived! In a moment, in that discrete moment, I felt relief, and relief, I have learned, is a highly underrated emotion. The world refreshened in a moment. I had returned to the world I knew, the world before I walked through Harvard Yard wanting to kill people. It seems to me that in that moment, I rose a few inches off the ground. I felt that a window to euphoria that had been closed for years was reopened. I floated; I felt lighter; I felt unbounded and untethered, released into a more bearable and greater light.

I was reminded of a test I had experienced in the eye doctor's office, when they expose your eyes to lenses of various shades of darkness and light. Some of the lenses are so dark you can barely see through them, while others are only lightly tinted. In that moment, I felt like I went two lenses up, into two greater degrees of lightness. And it stayed that way. It wasn't like it went away the next day. I know it may be hard to believe that the change was this clean, this precise. I am sure that there were psychosomatic factors; certainly my psychological readiness to accept the medications at that moment played a part and, who knows, may have made my brain more receptive to the chemical changes. But it felt like a solid change, a chemically defined transformation. Rigorous. Not flimsy. This was the informed, lasting, respectable change of science, of laboratories. This was my own personal paradigm shift, brought to me by the army of research scientists of Eli Lilly and Company.

With regard to the black thoughts . . . How shall I put this? With the Prozac, the thoughts never went away (for that to happen, I would have to forget them, which, of course, I was unable to do) but they held less sway over me. They melted somewhat. An attack of horrible thoughts used to feel like a steak knife going into my side. With the Prozac, the steak knife became a butter knife, and sometimes not even that. The thoughts still hurt, to be sure. I still thought of them daily, hourly, was aware of them all the time, but they didn't go as deep. And even when I did think them, I was more easily able to put them aside and get on with the task at hand. For the first time in years, I was really able to lose myself in something, whether it was work, watching a movie, or talking with a friend. If I were to put a number on it, which I really can't, I would say that Prozac has reduced my symptoms by 50 to 80 percent. But the immediacy of the relief it brought made it feel even more dramatic than that.

That whole summer I floated. My world had changed. Things were softer now. Over a three-month period, as Dr. Porter raised the medication from twenty to forty to sixty to eighty milligrams, I worked steadily at my film job, began working out daily, and lost fifteen pounds. I felt reborn, younger. And I won back Laura. She had developed a skepticism about me, that I was unavailable, unreliable, even untrustworthy—generous and creative and warm, but not necessarily the best person for the long haul. And, as she told me, she felt terrible about feeling this way. I was her first choice, she told me, if I could only . . . get it together. And so I showed her, relentlessly. Even when she was trying to get some distance on the situation, I called her several times a day, and in time I visited her, and wrote her cards and poems, and spent my last dimes on presents, and tried to be more direct with my feet on the ground. I showed her again, and again, and again my relentless and deep and undeniable love and affection and ability to change, even when she said time and time again that she wanted to be with me but couldn't. Our reuniting was sealed with a kiss on the Coney Island ferris wheel, Brooklyn and the Atlantic Ocean beneath us. Later, after she was accepted into a doctoral program in clinical psychology in northern New Jersey, she and I moved into the first-floor apartment of an old Victorian house in a Jersey town a few miles from the city . . . All of this, I owed to my own determination, and to Prozac.

But there was another side, inevitably — most notably a sort of mental vacuity that I had never before experienced. With the increase in dosage, it seemed my mind began to empty. For great stretches of time, I thought about nothing. In my younger and more vulnerable days, those many wasted days with Henry, it seemed there was never a moment during which there wasn't something going on in my brain — a constant wave of thought or mental activity. Words, sentences, visions, ideas, calamities — some of it wonderful, most of it horrible — but always, always, I was thinking of something. Now I went through great bouts of empty-mindedness. Riding the subway, I would miss my station by five stops before noticing it. I paused more when talking to people, more umms and ahhs and sentences that trailed off into nothing. I couldn't remember things I had just done — had I really locked the door, fed the dog, brushed my teeth a minute ago? I couldn't remember, and would have to go back and check. (Checking is another symptom of OCD.) I couldn't remember anybody's telephone number — before the Prozac, I was a walking Rolodex and could remember numbers I'd only called a few times. It was hard to focus on any serious task for more than a half-hour at a time. I had difficulty completing things. My thoughts, however purposeful initially, would melt into nothingness. It felt like I had been out in the sun too long. I felt like I had lost about ten IQ points.

I also needed to sleep more. When Henry was alive, I'd stay up until dawn and feel more alive at three in the morning than I had all day long. A month into the Prozac, I found myself needing to go to bed at nine thirty at night. I realized, over time — it took a long time before I became fully aware of this — I could no longer drink alcohol. Whereas booze had once produced in me an almost instant effervescence, now it induced only unpleasant metallic feelings, a feeling of depression. My mood would sour after half a drink. I tried different types of wine, beer, liquor — always, within half a drink, that awful metallic hopeless destructive feeling took over. With great reluctance, I gave up drinking.

But in all of this, there was no real choice about not continuing Prozac. I needed to float, and I needed to be numb. I chose to become comfortably numb. Over the years I have come to accept and embrace and love and adore it. I am entirely aware that what I am experiencing is a manufactured joy, fabricated in a lab somewhere in Indiana. But I don't give a damn how artificial, synthetic, manufactured, plastic my moods are. I don't care if my happiness is solely a neurological-biological-chemical creation. Joy is joy. Synthetic joy is still joy.

It should be said that, in time, I dutifully and nervously told Dr. Porter about all my worries, fears of erections and all that. He listened to me, calmly as always, and suggested to me that all my symptoms and theories were very much part of my obsessive-compulsive profile. I found it deeply reassuring that my crazy ideas could, by people experienced with these behaviors, be made sense of and be understood as part of a larger pattern. We also spent many sessions interpreting the meaning of my obsessions, the fact that, for example, perhaps I wanted to show the world my erection because I wanted to show off what I was capable of, my potency and talent and phallocentric ambitions. We did a lot of Freudian and analytic stuff. Eventually he referred me to a psychoanalyst, whom I saw on a daily basis for a period of two years. It cost a fortune. I figured out a lot of things about myself, and why I do certain things, and all my vulnerabilities and insecurities. Over time, my relationships improved; I became more assertive; I told people more often than I used to what was really on my mind. But as for addressing my most pressing needs, the reason why I went to see a psychiatrist in the first place — the reduction of intolerable symptoms of OCD — I would trade away all that hard-won insight for one capsule of Prozac.

During that first summer of Prozac, it was apparent to others that I was greatly changed. "You're the old Charlie," my father said to me one evening, about two months after I started the medication. I had just come back from a three-mile run and we were sitting on the patio, talking happily.

"Thank you," I said, as if I had anything to do with it.

   ⊸ ⊸ ⊸

But others were not lucky enough to enter the floating, pillow world with me. Three months after the Prozac gurgled so pleasantly through my brain, Mrs. Court drove her blue Volvo north to a farmhouse in the Berkshires:

It was fall, early fall. The leaves were just starting to turn. The woman was driving slowly because she was drunk. It was difficult to stay in the lane. She . . . what was the word? . . . she veered. Yes, she was veering. She had been veering for a long time.

It occurred to her vaguely, almost imperceptibly, that she could get a ticket for those two things, being drunk and driving too slowly. But so what if she got a ticket. What the hell was there to lose? Her license? Her reputation? Her career? But then again, she didn't want a ticket. That would impede the plan. She hasn't the time or the energy for a ticket. A ticket actually would be dreadful, one more disaster. She has work to do. She has to bridge a gap later today. She will embark on a grand experiment or journey . . . or perhaps just something painful and simple and real. The mountains around her (they were getting steeper now) were simple and clean. Soon everything would be clean. Suffering would end soon.

Nervous fingers on the steering wheel. The car (she could see the hood in front of her) was a blue Volvo and it handled the road well, even though she was drunk. (The ads are true, she thought, Volvos are safer, even when you're drunk.) Volvos help with veering. And she was not so familiar with the roads. She so rarely went to the farm. She had not been there since 1983. Not been back. But today she would go back for a rendezvous with her angel, the grievous angel. She had been too dumb to know it (same way dumb about Virginia Woolf), but her Henry/Angel had been a Shropshire lad from the start, a track manager dying young.

She felt excited to be approaching the farm. Not too long to wait now. Soon. The farm the only place she wanted to go now. Today she will rejoin her angel, he who was too pure and crazy for the world. The return of the grievous angel. Returning to the grievous angel. "The pure products of America go crazy," wasn't that a line from William Carlos Williams? Or Allen Ginsberg: "I saw the best minds of my generation destroyed by madness, starving hysterical naked." She thought of Virginia Woolf. Now she knew, really knew, how Virginia felt. Before all this (all this!) she had written learned articles about Virginia Woolf, she was considered by many people to be an expert, a scholar, an—hah!—an authority on Virginia Woolf (how fucking ridiculous) but, now she knew, drunkenly on the highway, that she knew nothing about Virginia then, but she knew everything about her now. Henry had taught her about Virginia Woolf. She was Virginia Woolf, heading for the waves. Henry had shown her the waves, the way to the waves.

Henry/Angel was better at technical things than she was. In another lifetime, Henry would have been an engineer, a manufacturer, a designer. She was intimidated by his example. How would she be able to duplicate it? But Henry would show her the way. Just a matter of timing. Timing the pill and the smoke. It was okay, okay, Henry would show her the way. Henry had always shown the way: NO REASON, nothing rational, no sense in analysis, in the end there was no thought, only blood and colors. Henry, she knew, was white when he died, powdery white, silver and pale (all at the same time) . . . well, she could be white, too.

Blood and colors. Blood and maybe rain. Blood and definitely rain. She saw a picture of herself, running. She was running around the farmhouse, the farmhouse that had never been hers, or Henry's, had belonged only to her former husband; she saw herself running in a large circle around the green farmhouse and it was raining and she was getting wet. But the rain was not water, it was blood, and it was soaking her and her pretty dress, it was covering it all—her arms, her legs, her hair, her dress—with redness and she had to (had to, was forced to, needed to) run under the eaves so as not to be fully covered with the red blood rain. Rain and Blood, Blood and Rain in the Berkshires.

Knew her death would be gruesome. Could only imagine what people would think. Palpable embarrassment at her funeral. People (once friends) not knowing what to say. A terribly awkward reception. Terribly awkward. Make people scared. People relieved when it was over. "How tragic," they would say. They would come and go, speaking of Michelangelo. Lay me out on ether. Etherize me. "How awful about Joyce," they would say. "How tragic, how awful." "So terrible." "Yes, so terrible." Hah!—she thought—she was doing better than she had in years. Around her the mountains were simple and clean.

At the house now. Pulling car up. No one else but her and Henry, no one else now, no one, all gone, only alcohol, pills, her, Henry, angels, clouds, into the sky, air, smoke, Volvo, war, shot up, shell shock, together now, together, end of something, end of pain, end of nausea, no dizziness, no craziness, everything clear.

Attach tube from exhaust pipe, route it into window, tape it up (as best you can.)—Take pills. Repeat as needed.

A song lyric from somewhere in her brain:

So much pain, I can't explain.

Stumbling drunk now. It's okay now. Okay, to stagger. No one watching. Stagger all you want. More Glenlivet. Drink from bottle. Only the best for her. Let it not be said at her wake that she didn't drink good scotch. Eulogy: "She drank the best scotch, and then she died." "She went to the dogs." "She was crazy." "She was in a lot of pain for a long, long time." They would try and make sense of it. Make it neat. Explain it, make it explainable, explicable. Many reasons for her behavior: let's look at them now, shall we? Shall we outline them on the blackboard, or are they already on the syllabus?

So much pain. She couldn't explain.

Where the hell was that lyric from, anyway?

Engine on now. Lightheaded, a little. Nothing would be neat. .. Nobody now. Henry only. No one else. Who cares about anyone else. Only him. Henry. Angel. Henry. Angel. Henry. Angel . . .

It was funny, she thought with surprising coherence, as fumes engulfed, she had once been a success . . .

⋰ ⋰ ⋰

When my parents called me in New York City to tell me that Joyce Court had killed herself, in the same place, in the exact same fashion, and at the same time of year as Henry had, I was horrified, but not at all surprised. This completes the gothic cycle, I thought. The series of events that started with Henry's overdose of pills in a bathroom in Cold River in 1979 had come to a conclusion. The circle was drawn, the cycle of pain over. Mr. Court would not come next, I knew. "Suicide is not in my repertoire," he had said to me once, not long after Henry died.

I never asked my parents or anybody else for further details about Joyce's death. All I knew were the simplest facts. No further explanation was necessary. I knew the three things I needed to know:

One, Henry did kill her off, in the end.

Two, I resolved then and there to simply extract anything related to Cold River from my existence. I would say good-bye to Cold River and all its miserable pathologies and suicidal characters. Part I of my life would be called Cold River, and that part was done. I would return there only when I had to, for obligatory visits to my parents on well-recognized holidays, and that would be it.

And three, I was entirely ready to leave behind, forever and ever amen, my tendency to associate with people who had a predilection for killing themselves.

seven

Islands of Functioning

And yet . . . it would not be so easy.

◆ ◆ ◆

Three years after Joyce Court died, I was nearing the completion of my graduate work at the art school at Columbia. I had been making a documentary about three homeless men. I followed the three men, who proclaimed themselves a sort of family, for three years as they moved from parks to abandoned buildings and back again. I spent hundreds, thousands of hours with them. I filmed them cooking, shaving, cutting their hair, smoking crack, taking care of their group of pet rats, and watching television on the sidewalk with a set plugged into the bottom of a street lamp. I took them back to the suburban towns where they had grown up, and filmed them touring the middle-class homes and respectable neighborhoods they had been raised in. For a while I all but lived with them in the candle-lit basement of an abandoned building near Union Square that was slowly being torn down. (A massive Virgin megastore and shiny new cineplex now exist on that spot.) After the building was demolished, I filmed them scratching through the rubble for their belongings, the Empire State Building looking on impassively in the back of the shot. I filmed them in an apartment they shared briefly after the oldest member turned sixty-five and suddenly received a $7,000 check from Social Security. (He cashed the check through my bank; the reason for the considerable sum, I learned upon investigation, was that alcoholism was suddenly deemed to be a reimbursable disability.) The three men represented different generations of homelessness: the oldest was a Bowery alcoholic (three pints of vodka a day); the middle one was a Vietnam veteran, an ex-heroin addict, and an ex–Times Square prostitute (he claimed to have briefly been a consort of Tennessee Williams); and the third was addicted to crack. I asked the middle one why they didn't stay in the city shelters. "Man, I already been in Vietnam," he responded emphatically.

It was a brutal, harrowing experience. At one point I was pricked inadvertently by one of their syringes. Although the needle didn't appear to have broken my skin, I worried for months that I might have contracted HIV. After putting it off for years, I tested negative. A female prostitute was found dead in the basement of the abandoned building, her face smashed in by a brick. The three men were questioned by a detective, and I in turn was questioned about the likelihood of their having perpetrated such an act. I testified, as I believed, that I didn't think they were involved. This event taught me the difference between the murderous "ideation" in my mind (as in Harvard Yard) and true murder. That difference was graphically underscored when I arrived the day after the murder to find a trail of dried blood leading down the stairs to the basement.

For all the hassle, the final product wasn't worth it. I struggled with the technical and financial aspects of filmmaking. A lot of the best material was missed because I didn't have a camera, or did have a camera and didn't capture scenes well. Beyond that, I realize now, the film was never really about its subjects. The real reason why I pursued the three homeless men with such a vengeance was that they were symbols, or puppets, for Henry, Nick, and me. I was enthralled by them because they were stand-ins, really, for my troubled friends and me. I had gone out seeking visceral and dramatic images of interior struggle, and I had found them. It was sort of a precursor, a dry run, to telling this story. I can see now that it was naïve and in fact in-sulting to my subjects that I should presume any connection between the difficulties of three privileged suburban boys and their troubles. Certainly I learned this by the project's end. By the end, I respected and valued the divisions between us. I learned that there is nothing to compare to being homeless, and that it had been a romanticization of their situation for me to regard it as anything different from what it was. At the completion of the film I was utterly drained. My credit cards were way over the limit; I was months behind on my rent. Laura had become understandably frustrated that I was spending most of my money on three homeless men and a project that dragged on for years.

For a short time anyway, as a way to regroup, I needed to get some steady work. I saw a job notice for a position as a case manager at a small agency that provided housing for adults with chronic mental illness and a history of homelessness, and on a whim I answered it. I had no qualifications for the position other than my work at group homes—and the fact that I had OCD, though of course I didn't mention that during the job interview, or at any other time during my employment. Mainly I wanted the job because it represented a regular paycheck and health insurance, unlike the freelance film projects I was used to. When I got the job, I was positive I would stay no longer than a year.

Of course none of it turned out that way.

ᦾ ᦾ ᦾ

Despite my almost complete lack of formal preparation, I felt I had seen enough of homelessness to know that those who are homeless are not like you and me—they generally come from brutally impoverished if not abusive backgrounds; they ingest copious amounts of street drugs; they have diseases like AIDS and hepatitis. At my new job I was expected to meet with my clients twice a week in their homes—in scattered apartments rented by the agency in Washington Heights, at the very northern tip of Manhattan. In the language of Medicaid, which funded our program, I was to provide for my clients "medication and symptom management," training in "daily living skills," and "substance abuse and crisis intervention services." I interpreted this to mean that I was supposed to show up, meet with them, and see what happened.

I was surprised to learn that about half of my twelve clients were from the same generally middle-class background that I was from. We'd read the same books, seen the same movies, been to the same schools. Two clients, before they developed schizophrenia and bipolar disorder, had been students at Wellesley and Cornell. Another had graduated from Colgate and read her poetry at gatherings in Soho. Another had been an importer-exporter of Indian goods before he became so depressed he could no longer function. I was particularly unsettled to learn that one of my charges was a fellow graduate student at Columbia. Karl was a brilliant physics student, and also diagnosed with chronic paranoid schizophrenia. He looked the part of the mad scientist—wild Einsteinian hair and a gleam in his eyes. He took many leaves of absence when the delusions took over, but always eventually returned to school, getting straight As. (A copy of his unblemished transcript was in his chart.) Karl had grown up in the town next to mine, he was just about my age, and his father was a professor, as mine was. It was all a little too close to home; I wanted a clear divider between the clients and me. A more specific point of comparison was that Karl's father was a professor of dentistry, and Karl's teeth were entirely rotted out. My father taught economics, and for most of my life I have been terrible with money. Karl and I both seemed to have passively rebelled against the careful professions of our fathers.

Shortly after I started the job, Karl told me he had plans to move out of his apartment. (Perhaps it was a coincidence, or perhaps Karl too wanted a clear divider.) He said he wanted to move to a YMCA in Bronx by the end of June. Karl never said so, but it was clear that he wanted a place where he would be left alone and not hounded by people like me asking about his medications and "daily living skills." We stood in his room as he told me reluctantly—I had to force it out of him—about his plans. His room definitely looked like the quarters of a crazy person: he had lived in it for seven years, but there was virtually nothing in it but books and notebooks of incomprehensible writing and formulas, and a half-dozen garbage bags filled with soiled clothes. There were cigarette burns in the rug and blankets and sheets. You didn't want to look under the bed for fear of what might be under there—probably at the very least bottles filled with urine. But the most amazing thing about the place was the walls. Once painted a rather pretty robin's-egg blue, the walls were now dark and gray, but inconsistently so. They were quite beautifully and richly smudged with the residue of cigarettes and, I think, mental illness. The only decoration was Karl's Columbia undergraduate diploma, which was summa cum laude. It was a fading and wrinkled scroll of paper attached to the wall by a single tack.

One afternoon Karl and I stood in front of that solitary piece of paper talking at length about diplomas. Karl felt the piece of paper meant nothing, an arbitrary formality created solely for the institution's own purposes and self-perpetuation. (He said it just like that—he spoke formally, using technical words.) I was inclined to agree with him, but I had just that week gotten my Columbia diploma after much struggle and was feeling happy about it. In that spirit, I tried to convince him that his diploma was a significant recognition of his intelligence and learning, one that ushered him into the company of educated people and announced to the world his expertise in a scientific field. Karl said nothing.

When Karl confirmed his moving-out plans by showing me a receipt for his first month's rent at the Y, I made a half-hearted effort to convince him not to go. He had an illness, I said, and he would benefit from my support and the structure of an agency. Karl didn't buy any of that and asked to sign his discharge papers relieving my agency of any further responsibility for him. He signed them in a flash. Awkwardly we shook hands, and he was gone. I realized afterward that, principally, I was relieved.

The next day I inspected his room. I feared the worst (an afternoon dealing with bottles of urine), but the books and notebooks and garbage bags were gone, the floors were swept, and the place, remarkably, even smelled fresh. It appeared as if he had used actual cleaning products. The smudges on the wall were still there, but they were irradicable without numerous coats of paint. Karl had left only one thing: on the wall, untouched, was the diploma. I was sure that he had left it for me. But why? As a refutation of my argument? As a gift? An affront? I'll never know. I took the diploma down, kept it in the office for a year, and then reluctantly threw it in the trash. So Karl had won in the end.

◆ ◆ ◆

But it was not Karl but a man named Michael Jasny, with whom I had far less in common, who affected me the most. I'm not sure why exactly—it may have been simply because I liked him very much. (I've since learned that there are two types of deeply troubled people: those who inflict their pain on others, and those who do not. Perhaps to his detriment, Michael was emphatically in the latter group.) Though he was twice my age and from another country, there was something in his tweedy diffidence and tendency toward half-baked abstraction that reminded me very much of Henry, and for that matter of myself. He was also exactly my height and build, and when I stood next to him, I saw my own body thirty years hence. I can also see that in my relentless pursuit of Michael's story, I was responding to the vexing mystery of Henry's death. At least with Michael, there was evidence.

It was an unusually hot day in April when I first visited Washington Heights to see Michael. The kids had opened the fire hydrants, spraying jets of water over the street, and a Mister Softee ice cream truck played the same mindless jingle over and over again. Michael always loved "the Heights," for reasons I didn't understand until much later. It was improbable, this displaced quiet Czech man living in the salsa-and-merengue-flavored area at the tip of Manhattan, spiritually much closer to the Bronx than to gleaming Midtown to the south. But I was to learn that perhaps one reason to appreciate the neighborhood was because the hospital was just a few blocks away—a huge medical center that looms over the area like an eerie monolithic fortress. Michael used its services for a few weeks most years in April, when he evaluated his life (his birthday was in April) and typically went into a psychotic episode.

"Hello, you are right on time," Michael said, opening the door to his apartment. "Please come in. Would you like something to drink—cherry soda, perhaps?"

The man who stood in front of me appeared to be in his late fifties. He spoke in an utterly flat, almost mechanical monotone. He was about my height (well over six feet), with a once powerful, now somewhat plumpish build, and had the air of a distracted, unkempt former professor. He wore an old tweed jacket and a dark shirt and trousers.

If the neighborhood felt like the Dominican Republic, the apartment was completely out of time and space. It was a gray, drab place—peeling paint, dust balls in the corners. The sitting room was virtually empty, graced only with a luridly colored shag carpet, a mismatched sofa and chairs, a tacky glass-covered coffee table, and a couple of posters depicting generic nature scenes stuck haphazardly to the wall. My guess is the posters were provided by a previous, well-meaning case manager and were supposed to instill positive emotions in those who viewed them.

The floorboards creaked as I walked through the apartment and sat on the sofa.

Michael reappeared with the soda and three-by-five index card. He handed the card stiffly to me. On it was written:

Milosz "Michael" Jasny

Date of birth: 4-18-40

Psychiatrist: Dr. Victor Henley

Therapist: Valerie Reynolds

Medications: Depakote
              Prolixin
              Lithium
              Cogentin

"If you have any further questions about my case, please call my therapist, Ms. Reynolds," he said pointedly, in that mechanical voice. It was clear that was all he wanted to say about psychiatric matters.

We sat on the couch and I talked to him about the only thing I knew about Czechoslovakia: the books of Milan Kundera, whose novels, particularly *The Unbearable Lightness of Being*, had made a great impact on me. To my surprise, Michael said that he and Kundera had briefly been part of the same student revolutionary circles in Prague in 1968. "But I wasn't really a revolutionary," he said with a pained grin. "I was a capitalist, and that is why I came to the United States."

I asked him about his daily schedule. In his flat, detached way—it was as if he were speaking about somebody else—he said, "I wake up at 7 a.m., I leave for the program at 8:15 a.m., and I am at the day program at the hospital from 9 a.m. to 3 p.m. When I come home I take a short nap. On Tuesdays and Thursdays I meet with my case manager to discuss my personal problems. I make dinner at 6 p.m. I read or work on some projects, and I go to bed at 9:30 p.m. On weekends I pursue leisure activities like walking or going to the movies. I am very good with my finances—you will not need to help me with that." Indeed he was; I learned in time that he sent several thousand dollars a year to his sister in Czechoslovakia, saved from his $600-a-month Social Security check.

The next day I read Michael's chart in the agency's office. The records stated that he had been a leading engineering student and top athlete, a swimmer, in Prague, winning a scholarship to the university. He married, served in the military in an intelligence division, and worked as a research scientist at the Institute of Economics at the Czechoslovakian Academy of Sciences. In 1968 he defected to the United States, leaving his wife behind. He enrolled as a doctoral business student at New York University. Before he finished his dissertation, he was hired by one of the largest banks in the country. He became a vice president of the bank, the leader of something called a "Decision Analysis Team," and was remarried to a fellow Czech émigré, who was an engineering professor at Columbia. They lived on Central Park West and took annual winter vacations in the Caribbean and Hawaii. It was hard to reconcile all this with the person I had met—I was alarmed to read of the "level of functioning" (more Medicaid parlance) from which Michael had fallen.

"I believe his psychotic break occurred in 1976," Mrs. Reynolds, the therapist, said when I called her. "His father, to whom Michael was very close, was dying that year of heart trouble and cancer in Prague, and repeatedly wrote Michael asking to see him before he died. But as a defector, Michael couldn't go back. From what I understand, he started acting bizarrely at work, getting carried away with delusional ideas. His hygiene deteriorated; eventually, he stopped going to work. Around the same time that he was fired, his wife left him—I think she moved to Boston and got a job at M.I.T. He lived on his savings for some time—a year or so. After being evicted from his apartment, he lived in a hotel in Fort Lee, near the George Washington Bridge. After the money ran out, he worked as a janitor at a yeshiva in the Bronx. Finally he became homeless, and ultimately he was arrested and hospitalized."

According to Ms. Reynolds, Michael came to believe that he urgently needed to join the CIA, thinking that his international background uniquely qualified him for such work. He also thought that as a requirement for joining the CIA, he needed to be arrested. Acting on that delusion, he broke into a branch of the bank he used to work for. To ensure he would be arrested for this act, he called the police beforehand. He was jailed at Riker's Island and after a few months transferred to Manhattan State Psychiatric Hospital. He was there for a couple of years and then came to live at the agency in 1984. "The signs of his psychiatric decompensation are highly idiosyncratic," Valerie said. "It begins with sleeplessness. Then he starts to pace, smiles inappropriately, talks much more than usual, and drinks large amounts of orange juice."

"I'll watch out for the orange juice," I said.

"You'll like working with him," Valerie Reynolds said. "He's a fine man, a gentleman."

⋄ ⋄ ⋄

That spring Michael and I met twice a week, both in his apartment and at the student center at Columbia, since his day program was nearby. While undergraduates studied organic chemistry and played Frisbee on the lawn, Michael and I drank coffee and talked. Occasionally he told me about his "condition," as he called it. He never mentioned the name of his illness, although I think he did say once that "the doctors call it schizoaffective disorder," as if that was their opinion and they were entitled to it, no matter how misguided they were. (Schizoaffective disorder is a psychotic disorder marked by hallucinations and delusional beliefs as well as unstable moods.) Michael made no further mention of schizoaffective disorder, a diagnosis that had clearly been made by all of Michael's long string of psychiatrists over the years. Instead he described a mysterious debilitating ailment that had simply arrived one day and, essentially, poisoned his brain. He often complained of "not being able to concentrate." One day I brought him a Kundera novel and suggested we read it. "Oh no, thank you, Charles," he said, "I would not be able to follow it." He said he used to read the *New York Times* every day, and on weekends read the entire Sunday edition from cover to cover. "But I can't do it anymore—it is too stimulating for me," he said with that sad smile. Valerie told me that at one point Michael was assigned the task of writing a three-page manual for new patients at the day program. Michael worked assiduously on it for months and then resigned, saying he couldn't focus his mind. He did say that he could still listen to music. He particularly liked Anton Dvorak and his New World Symphony. "It is one man's document of his passage to America. I can relate to that," he told me.

But Michael never told me about the delusional thinking I had read about in the charts, the episodes during which he felt he could stop the famines in Africa or was the inventor of extraordinary new technologies. He never told me about the manic episodes that landed him in the hospital almost every year—perhaps, as he once confided to me, he couldn't remember them. No, the Michael I met with on the Columbia campus was eminently rational and calm. Clinton had recently been elected, and Michael, interested in politics, talked to me sanely and intelligently about the issues of universal health care and gays in the military. I was shocked when Valerie told me that Michael believed he had controlled the election.

I was tempted on any number of occasions—particularly at those moments of "connection" between us, after we had spent a pleasant hour or so talking—to reveal to Michael my own psychiatric history. I suppose I thought it might be helpful to him. He looked up to me, in his way, and perhaps my telling him that I'd had problems would have surprised him and even given him some unexpected hope. Or then again, perhaps not. All I know is I'm glad I didn't. It would have been extraneous: it was my understanding, and his, that I was there to do a job, not be his friend or intimate, and playing with those roles might have confused him. Actually I think it might have made him even more vulnerable. He looked to me for structure and guidance, and telling him about my own problems would have given him even less clarity than he already had.

And it wasn't just Michael that I wanted to "self-disclose" to. I felt that way about all my clients, some of whom I think would have found my revelations very beneficial. Again, I chose not to, out of reserve and embarrassment, and also because I didn't want to raise these issues with my supervisors. But the desire remained. I always felt slightly dishonest in my dealings with my clients. In one of my early visits to one of my client's apartments, I had taken out my wallet to give him my business card. Later, on the bus home, I opened my wallet and found that my Prozac prescription and the bill from my psychiatrist, which included my diagnosis, were missing. In a panic, I realized I must have left them behind in the client's apartment. What would happen if he found them? I didn't know what to do, and so did nothing. When I visited the client's apartment the next time, I found my papers lying innocently in the corner behind the armchair I'd been sitting in. It didn't look as if he had seen them. I retrieved them, relieved. Reflecting on this incident, though, I realized that some part of me wanted my client to find them, so I'd be forced to come clean.

But here's the thing: I saw, in working with Michael and my other clients, that I was good at this work. It all came exceedingly naturally—far more naturally than, for example, writing or documentary filmmaking. I responded to my clients, and they responded to me. I may have some natural abilities in reaching clients, but at the very heart of my rapport was my own experience with obsessive compulsive disorder. While I never revealed the diagnosis to the clients, and am thankful I did not, it informed everything I did with them and allowed me to understand their craziness. I related to their madness—I could understand how someone as rational and intelligent as Michael Jasny could be completely taken over by an irrational universe. I had lived in their country.

My colleagues, most of whom were far more educated and experienced in the field than I was, typically did not have this grasp. They would be more likely to instruct clients than to listen to them. Often it was those with the most education and clout, the psychiatrists, who had the least understanding. It is largely because I felt my skills were derived from my unique experiences, and not from any form of erudition, that I have resisted going back to school to get a degree in social work or psychology. Rightly or wrongly (certainly wrongly as far as my paycheck goes), I feel I have already received more than enough preparation in the field of mental health.

To be sure, though, overidentifying with clients can be problematic, if not dangerous. Certainly, it is a cliché in the mental health world that many people who enter it do so to work out their own problems. This is a cliché that I have never been comfortable with, perhaps because it so directly applies to me. The trick is to know that you can relate to clients in their general sense of dislocation, but to avoid specifically embracing, or endorsing, their pathology. Fitzgerald—as always, my literary compass—wrote famously: "The test of a first-rate intelligence is the ability to hold two opposed ideas in the mind at the same time, and still retain the ability to function." It is exactly that knack that is required to work effectively with psychotic people: you must hear and understand as best you can their version of distorted reality, while remaining stably in your world. Many of my colleagues would try one way or another to argue clients out of their psychotic beliefs, which is as pointless as telling an alcoholic all the fine reasons that he or she should not drink. On those rare occasions when we broached his illness, Michael ended the discussion with a stock line. "But I am not unhappy that I have a disability," he would say. "It has given me a different perspective on things. I am able to pursue my own projects, even do volunteer work. Sometimes I am almost glad I have a disability." I doubted that. Once a month he went to lectures at the New York Academy of Science, and for a few years he volunteered on the Washington Heights community board. But his explanation, stated exactly in the same way each time, had about it the feel of a carefully prepared position paper, delivered to generations of case managers and therapists before me.

◦ ◦ ◦

In the early 1990s, the mayor of New York City and the governor of New York signed an unprecedented initiative to address homelessness in New York City. The tide of homelessness had been rising through the 1980s, fueled triply by AIDS, crack cocaine, and the emptying of psychiatric facilities. The New York agreement established three thousand permanent beds for formerly homeless adults with mental illness. The recipients of these beds would live "in the community," either in rented apartments or in community residences with supportive services. Almost overnight my little agency doubled in size. The new initiative meant that we could offer Michael and other longtime clients in our agency permanent apartments in a comfortable building on the Upper East Side, near the East River. Michael's Washington Heights apartment building was labeled "transitional" by the state's mental health office, meaning that occupants were meant to be "rehabilitated" within three to five years and then moved on to independent living.

In the staff meeting that week, I seem to remember we talked about Michael for all of about three minutes. It was a "cut-and-dried" case. If anybody was suited for the new apartments, it was Michael. His illness was chronic and required permanent support. And Michael was somebody the agency was comfortable offering an open-ended lease to: never "a management problem," he wouldn't be one to not pay his rent or not take care of the place. I felt a ripple of discomfort as we made the decision. I knew from my own life how disruptive change was. For someone as unstable as Michael, a move could be infinitely unsettling. But I stifled those qualms and nodded my assent.

I came to Michael with the good news. I explained that the new apartment would come with brand-new Pottery Barn furniture, it would be in a far nicer neighborhood, and it would be near cultural opportunities like the Academy of Sciences and museums. Most important, he could stay there as long as he lived. Michael listened and nodded and smiled one of those anguished grins. As if to please me, he mechanically repeated back to me all the rational reasons for the move. But I sensed deep misgivings that were buried deep inside him, grave doubts that he was too polite to express. At a later visit, he did haltingly raise his concerns. I listened carefully and then told him again all the reasons why the move would be so good for him.

We moved Michael in the first days of July, during a hot spell of hundred-degree days. Unlike some other agency clients who were moving to the new apartments, Michael had virtually no belongings: two garbage bags of clothes, ten boxes of books and papers, and that was all. He explained that he had donated anything extraneous to the Salvation Army. The move went smoothly enough, despite the heat, and in the weeks that followed, Michael appeared to settle into his new apartment. He paid his new roommate a hundred dollars so he could take the larger bedroom. I continued to visit him twice a week.

Two months after the move, I got a call from an emergency room physician at a city hospital a few blocks away from Michael's new apartment. The doctor wanted to know what medications he took. The police had brought him, badly bruised and scraped, to the ER after they had fished him out of the East River at daybreak. A jogger had seen him flailing about in the water and called the police. In the ER, Michael was being restrained because he was so agitated. I told the doctor about Michael's psychiatric condition. He was treated on the medical unit for a day, since tests indicated an electrolyte imbalance in his kidneys, and then transferred to Psychiatry. One doctor speculated that his mania might have been triggered by the problem with his kidneys.

No amount of training prepares one for experiencing the derangement of a person in the midst of a full-blown manic episode. The Michael I had known bore slight resemblance to the flailing, shouting, and entirely psychotic person I saw the next day. "OHHELLO CHARLES, HOW AREYOU, ISIT CHARLES, YESITIS CHARLES, YES, YES!" Michael said when I visited him on the unit. He was tied to the bed with rubber tubes. There was a gash on his head. He rushed all the words together, without pause. "IAMSOGLAD TOSEEYOU, MAYBEYOU CANHELP!!!" he shouted. "IMUST GETTOAFRICA SOON! NOW!!! THENECESSARY SATELLITE TECHNOLOGY HAS ARRIVED, BYRADAR YESTERDAY! THEPOPE HASINVITEDME TOSAVE ALLTHOSE INBOTSWANA. MY PLAN, IMMIGRANTSONLY, ARRIVES TOMORROW BY PRIORITYMOST IMPORTANT MAIL!!! THEPLAN ARRIVESTOMORROW!!! I AMREADY TO HELP!!!" An hour-long monologue ensued, which I was powerless to interrupt, about numerous international rescue missions and stunning technological feats that he needed to accomplish. After some time, I was able to detect a sort of pattern to his manic diatribe: in his scrambled way he said he was being monitored by satellites and that, as a pioneering immigrant, his actions had important ramifications for all immigrants who followed him. He seemed to think that if he was successful, those who followed him would succeed as well; but if he failed, it would spell doom for everybody else. Trying to get back to some kind of reality, I asked him why he had jumped in the river. It was, he explained in a crazed fifteen-minute burst of words, an attempt to rescue a woman's radio. "IHEARD ON 1010 WINSAM RADIO—YOULISTEN TOIT I KNOW CHARLES, TRAFFIC ISIMPORTANT—THATA WOMAN LOST HERRADIO IN THE EASTRIVER. I NEEDEDTO RESCUE IT FORHER!!!"

I wondered if Michael's past as a competitive swimmer had anything to do with his jumping in the river. I had learned by then that even the most psychotic behavior is rarely without some basis in reality. Valerie Reynolds agreed. "I remember he told me once that as a boy he used to dive into rivers and lakes from great heights, on a dare. He used to swim daily at a pool in Harlem. There was actually a shooting there. It didn't stop him from going—he told me he didn't mind, because there were less people there afterward!"

The psychiatrist at the hospital was a very nice man from Haiti and spoke absolutely no English, at least that I could understand. He looked at me quizzically when I explained that Michael's diagnosis was schizoaffective disorder. Nonetheless he pumped him with large doses of antipsychotics and "mood stabilizers."

Gradually they took effect. I visited him every week for three months, and each week he was more sedated and seemingly rational. Eventually he was completely back to his detached self and mechanical way of speaking. Toward the end of his stay, on a warm October afternoon, we went on a pass to visit his apartment. The idea was to slowly reintegrate him into the world beyond the inpatient unit, but I had brought the wrong key and we had to sit on the front steps. I ran down the street and bought some coffee and grapes, and we sat on the steps for a couple of hours inhaling the sunlight. We didn't talk about therapy or medications or psychosis. Actually, we talked about Volkswagens. I had just bought an ancient VW Beetle, and Michael had had one in Czechoslovakia. He drew a sketch on a piece of paper and explained to me how the engine worked. That wasn't the last time I saw Michael, but that's the way I like to remember him.

As part of our agency's expansion, we broke ground on a community residence to serve twenty-five additional patients. Not long after Michael got out of the hospital, I took the job of managing the new facility. Michael and I spent weeks discussing my departure. He said he was upset but that he had seen many case managers come and go and that he would adjust. I told him that we would stay in touch, and that he could always contact me in a crisis. He gave me a gift of two expensive pens and told me to stay on top of my paperwork in my new job.

A month later, in November 1994, George Pataki became governor of New York. Upon taking office the following January, he attempted to slash funding for community mental health programs by about 25 percent across the board. The eventual cuts were not quite that deep, but in early 1995 a number of outpatient programs were either closed or restructured. One of them was Michael's program with Valerie Reynolds.

Michael was told on a Tuesday in February that his program was going to change beyond recognition. In keeping with trends in managed mental health care, the program was going to serve patients only on a time-limited basis, six months to a year. It would be much more focused on the tangible outcomes of its services, such as increased measures of patients' daily functioning. Long-term patients, like Michael, would be referred to low-demand clinics that were less treatment centers than drop-in centers for patients to socialize with their peers. There would be no therapists or doctors there; for his medications, Michael would check in with a doctor at the hospital for a few minutes a month and get new prescriptions. He would, of course, no longer be a patient of Ms. Reynolds's.

Four days later Michael left an envelope containing $1,500 with the name of the executive director of my agency on it. Otherwise he left his belongings as they were. He was last seen by his roommate. Michael said to him, "I have to come up with some new ideas," and walked out the door.

Within a few days, Michael's new case manager filed a missing person's report with the police. A detective examined the apartment for foul play, claiming the packet of $1,500 as "evidence." Alerts were posted at precincts and emergency rooms around the city. We checked in regularly with our contacts at psychiatric hospitals, and checked the Medicaid and Social Security databases. There was no activity. We checked with Michael's bank and discovered that $400 in savings remained untouched. We called the morgue and medical examiner's office regularly. They had nothing that matched our report. Weeks went by and nothing happened.

Valerie and I were in constant touch, and we both sadly agreed that Michael was almost certainly dead—that having jumped in the river once, he probably jumped again, this time with a different result. But no body ever turned up.

⋄ ⋄ ⋄

Nobody quite knew what to do with Michael's papers. They sat in the office for a couple of months. Finally one day I paged through them awkwardly, feeling like I was going through the diary of a dead man. There were hundreds upon hundreds of pages, filled with manic handwriting, and almost all completely unintelligible. There were odd signs and symbols. A dollar bill was pasted on one page. On another: "The war ended, 1:53 a.m. and 27 seconds, May 13th 1993. The war has ended." Slightly more coherent were drawings and schemes of engines and game show proposals sent to and rejected by the networks.

I didn't left myself think it at the time, but a pulse of excitement went through me as I read the diaries. I felt awkward and brazen at the same time, realizing I was going somewhere that I probably had no right to go, but also detecting the scent of a trail. Unlike Henry, whose death remains a disturbing mess to me, Michael had left behind evidence. I brought the journals home, and in my study over the next few days I spent hours sifting through the hundreds of pages of psychotic ramblings and inventions and ideas and nonsense. On a piece of paper I wrote down all the coherent, sane passages I could find. This is their sum total:

I had obsessions in childhood, which I would not discuss.

We were well off. Family did not suffer until the end of the war when food was scarce and I spent long weeks in a bomb shelter.

Arrival [in America] in Nov 68

I had to invent myself

Give us your educated, your gifted, your energetic few, and we will help them achieve.

Give us your educated. Do or die. Do or be damaged.

April 76: first class Pan Am 747 from London to NY. Relaxed. Within a month my father would die of heart

A constant theme of the notebooks was something called Solaris Island. Finally I came across a proposal for Solaris Island, sent to the Ford Foundation and a dozen others:

Today is Winter Solstice. It is a good day to think about the sun. It is also a good day to present an opportunity. The opportunity is building, maintaining, and operating a new type of facility . . . a facility with the descriptive and resonant name of Solaris Island. The facility does not have to be built overnight. Perhaps in the first phase, it could be a ship equipped with the latest in solar technology. . . . In the second phase, it could become a facility built on those protruding rocks in the New York Harbor. . . . Maintaining and operating the facility as a multicultural working, educational and visitor center would be a major challenge. . . . Two things are certain: Solaris Island would create jobs and educational opportunities.

This proposal has a deeper, personal meaning. On this day, twenty years ago, I was admitted to the U.S. as a permanent resident. On that day . . . I was given the green light to live and work in the U.S. "to pursue happiness." . . . Czechoslovakia was not forgotten, but it became a starting place on a journey that now includes America.

Michael had carefully filed away all the polite rejection notices that the proposal had received.

In the last of his notebooks, I found specific references to death and suicide:

Death: valium and alcohol

I am dying incognito

Last message: It is better to die than to live
unfulfilled life . . . a life of pain. I blame only
myself for my death. It could not be prevented.

Obsession: swim towards Solaris Island

The last notebook, no. 15, was the shortest. In its final passage I found the following sequence, written and rewritten many times, in Czech and in English:

Today I am 55 years old. April 18 is my birthday. It is also the
day of my death. I will drown in the East River.

Out of the water I came, into the water I return

I am sacrificing my life so that the idea of SOLARIS ISLAND
may soar

THE END. I WILL DROWN TODAY. SORRY FOR THE MESS.

Putting the notebooks away, I cried. I cried and I cried and I cried. I cried for Michael, and—I think—I cried for Henry.

Michael's death having been confirmed for me, I felt wrenches of horrendous guilt. I—we—the system—the governor of New York—didn't listen to him. Michael clearly forecast his fate for us, and we stayed within our rational worlds and didn't hear what he knew was best for him. We thought he was crazy when he was sane. I might have helped him, but I did nothing. I was the "good employee," went with the flow. I got Michael moved efficiently and quickly. I got stuff done, got tasks taken care of. And the consequences? That was not for me to worry about. But reading those diaries, I realized that I couldn't have done anything about New York State budget policy, but I could have spoken up for my Michael. Reading that diary, I felt that Michael's blood was on my hands. I still feel that way sometimes. Writing about him and holding on to his diaries have been ways to hold on to him, and make myself feel it was not all in vain.

The next day I called Valerie and told her what I found.

⋄ ⋄ ⋄

We kept in touch with the police and the emergency rooms. But after hearing nothing for a year, the agency filled his apartment with a new client. Michael's diaries sat in boxes under my desk. For some reason I looked at them again one day and found a rare coherent note from a 1981 entry: "My best friend in the U.S.—Zilmos Novak, 1324 Riverside Drive, New York, New York." I called telephone information—no listing at that address. But some time later, in a New Jersey phone book, I found a listing for a Zilmos Novak about a mile from my home. It had to be the same man. I called him one night, nervously. After some confusion, we established that we had known the same Michael Jasny, just at vastly different times in his life.

We met a few days later on the steps of the public library in my town. When I saw the large bearlike man climbing the steps toward me, I knew right away it was Michael's friend. He looked like Michael, if a much more intact version.

We went to a nearby café. Dr. Novak produced a picture of a confident, lean young man sitting at a picnic table. The man had thick, wavy hair and long sideburns. He wore sunglasses and a polo shirt, under which the lines of a muscular chest were visible. He was smiling, laughing really, with an irreverence that seemed to say that all was right in the world. I puzzled over the picture for a while, amazed. Then I showed Dr. Novak a picture I had brought with me, a Polaroid from Michael's chart. In a shabby apartment stood a man well into his fifties with thinning hair, some broken teeth, and a pronounced belly. His complexion would best be described as a dull gray. But most disturbing was his smile—pained and off-kilter, the smile of a mental patient.

I think we both wondered if there had been some mistake. Had we really known the same person? We placed the photographs side-by-side, and after some minutes we could see that the curve of the jaw line and the shape of the remaining teeth were identical in each picture. It was the same man. It was as if we were comparing a victim's dental records after a plane crash. For the next two hours we sat in the café, transfixed, telling stories of our two different versions of the same man.

Dr. Novak, a business professor, told me his version of Michael, a brilliant, reckless young man. They met in the Czech army in the early 1960s. Based on IQ scores, they were assigned to the intelligence division, where they worked on computer prototypes. "I was a little younger than him and far less experienced in the ways of the world. I sort of tagged along for the ride," Novak said. He described Michael as someone who rarely did his requisite work, who often partied all night and was obsessed with women. He spent as much time as possible drinking and whoring, but then would come to class or work the next morning and dominate it with his ideas and charm. His ability to absorb information was legendary, Novak said, and when absorbed in something, he could work on a project for two or three days in a row, without sleeping. He was always slightly disheveled, his shirttail hanging out, and his ideas would often get far-fetched. In other words, he was a "bullshit artist" who usually got away with it, Novak said.

"I came first to the U.S., and then I sponsored Michael to come over. I was away for a while in upstate New York, but eventually I came to the city to teach, and we did many things as couples with his wife and mine. For a while Michael was doing well at the bank."

"When did you last see him?" I said.

"At the Brooklyn docks. He had started to crack up by then. He looked bad and was missing work. He talked about black spots and things like that. He came to stay with me for a few weeks and hardly got out of bed. I was going to Europe on sabbatical for a year, and he helped me load my trunks on a cargo ship. The last time I saw him was when he drove away in his Mercedes coupe. That was fifteen years ago. I looked for him for years. More so in the beginning. But I never heard anything about him, until you called the other day. To think, all this time, he was just five miles away. Now the puzzle is solved, sort of. Thank you for getting in touch with me."

I thought I detected moisture in his eyes.

⚜ ⚜ ⚜

There is a rather dated term in psychiatry, "islands of functioning," defined as "areas of intact functioning amid global impairment." It always puzzled me how Michael could be so acute in his observations of politics, for example, and then at the same time feel he was controlling elections. I couldn't integrate the polarities of his mind, how his ideas could be so crazy and so coherent at the same time. (But I shouldn't have been at all surprised—I suffer from the same combination of coherence and craziness.)

About a year after he disappeared, a colleague of Ms. Reynolds's saw, from afar in the subway, a large, messy, distracted-looking man. She was "90 percent sure it was Michael." Valerie and I didn't think so. Perhaps out of a certain self-protectiveness, we didn't want to hang on to fragile hopes. We were sure he had swum in the East River so Solaris Island could live. We were sure he was a victim of people like me who knew what was in his best interest.

There is a little barnlike structure sitting on a grassy patch by the East River at 96th Street. It is not far from the islands in the river that Michael wrote about. The building is about fifteen feet from the highway; probably a hundred thousand people drive by it every day and never notice it. One morning I read the sign on top of it. In bold letters it said something like Solar Power Demonstration Project—City of New York. With a kind of elation, I thought, "Solaris Island lives!"

A few days later I drove past the house again to get the exact name of the project. A crew of construction workers was tearing it down. Only the scaffolding remained.

eight

Songs from the Black Chair

Amid the almost uninterrupted prosperous sheen of Midtown Manhattan there are small blemishes—especially the closer you get to the corner of East 30th Street and First Avenue, site of the Bellevue shelter and home of my black chair. Outside the gleaming multiplex theater on East 31st and Second Avenue, for instance, you might see a man speaking to himself. Or you might see another man looking extraordinarily disheveled, who just happens to be doing vigorous and manic pull-ups from the walk signal attached to a telephone pole. And the closer you get to the corner of 30th Street and First Avenue, the greater the incidence of untoward and inappropriate behaviors you encounter. You might see, for instance—as I did on my way to work at the Bellevue shelter one night—a man drinking a beer and pissing at the same time. Or you might have to step over puke on the sidewalk, not once but twice or even three times within the space of one block. Or you might see a relatively sedate and normal-looking person, quietly standing in front of a deli, scream out abruptly and with no apparent provocation, "I wish someone would just shoot me—now!"

The prosperous residents of Murray Hill—those occupants of the handsome brownstones and brand-new high-rises—earnestly join forces and make valiant efforts to rid themselves of the repeated aesthetic insults that the endless stream of homeless men headed for the Bellevue shelter inflict on their neighborhood. The good citizens create "neighborhood coalitions" and "shelter task forces," and they put signs out on their sidewalks imploring passersby not to "water their plants"—that is, not piss on them. For years such organized opposition to the shelter has been going on, but to no apparent avail. Elaborate plans have been drawn up, and approved by the city government, to ship the whole operation out to Flatbush, Brooklyn, or some other suitably poor and downtrodden part of the city. Maybe the removal of the Bellevue shelter will happen someday, but for now it seems here to stay. The residents of Murray Hill seem unable to rid themselves of the shelter and its wretchedness. The vapors of homelessness seem to be permanently embedded in the landscape. But even if the massive, dark, gothic, ten-story, block-wide shelter were razed at some point in the future, and the site developed into one of those shiny apartment complexes, I think there would still be something not quite right about this place. Desperation will always be drawn to the corner of East 30th and First Avenue, and no amount of money or resolve will extinguish it.

The simple reason the shelter is so hard to extinguish is that it remains a vital and popular destination, at least for a certain type of tourist in New York: the homeless tourist. Twenty thousand men a year come to the shelter, for a night or for a lifetime. And about a thousand of those—those with psychiatric and pressing medical illnesses, the neediest of the needy, the most vulnerable of the vulnerable—are sent to see me and my team of social workers in our cramped back office for "assessment." What that really means is that we talk to them about what they're up to, and see what, if anything, we can do for them. (The men usually leave unhappy, because they don't generally get to stay at the Bellevue shelter but are shipped out to satellite shelters in the outer boroughs.)

A thousand men a year come and sit in the black chair next to my desk. They are between eighteen and eighty years old, usually black or Hispanic, usually with a psychiatric condition and a substance-abuse history (crack, heroin, and alcohol), often with a forensic history (usually released from prison that day), and quite often with a major disease. At some point, I always end up asking: "Are you hearing voices?" "What do the voices say?" "Have you ever seen things that other people didn't see?" "Have you ever tried to hurt yourself?" "Are you having thoughts of hurting yourself now?" A few times a month I hear responses like "I thought for about an hour today about jumping in front of the subway," or "I want to die," or "I can't tell you whether I'm going to hurt myself or not," or I am shown wrists that have recently been cut, or bellies and limbs and necks that have long scars in them. When I hear or see these things, I calmly tell the person in the black chair that I think he needs to go to the hospital in order to be safe. Almost always he agrees without complaint. I call 911 and write a note addressed to the attending psychiatrist, Bellevue Hospital emergency room, detailing my observations and an assessment of their mental status. Fortunately the hospital is only a block away. Within ten minutes, the police and EMTs arrive. "Good luck," I always say to the men as they are taken away. To my amazement, they almost always say, "Thank you."

For the records the staff and I are instructed to place the men we see into one or more of the following official categories of disability or distress, as promulgated by the city's health department:

SPMI (seriously and persistently mentally ill)
MICA (mentally ill chemical abuser)
Axis II (personality disordered)
Medical
Forensic (released from jail or prison)
Over 60 Years Old
Mentally Retarded/Developmentally Disabled
Immigrant
Physically Disabled
Vocational Problems
Domestic Situation

It's a nice list of bureaucratic categories, and it means nothing, really. I've created my own list. These, I've learned in my two years of sitting next to the black chair, are far more descriptive and pertinent descriptions:

The Travelers and the Wanderers
Guided by Voices
Vietnam Vets
Waylaid Tourists, Usually Recently Robbed
Criminals
"No English" and No Papers

Various Persons Destroyed by Alcohol, Crack, Heroin, or
   Other Substance
Alzheimer's Patients and Other Victims of Senility
Manic in America
People Who Choose to Live Underground and in Darkness
The Truly Weird, for Whom We Can Find No Category That Fits

But I keep all this to myself. I sit at the computer and duly check off the city's official list.

Of course, they are all travelers and wanderers. They come from Jamaica, Georgia, Colombia, Kuwait, Poughkeepsie, Italy, Oregon, Taiwan, Wyoming, Poland, Detroit, and Bosnia. And it is Manhattan—not Brooklyn, Queens, or the Bronx—that they want to come to.

      ◦ ◦ ◦

Countless times I've been caught in the middle of this exchange:

"Brooklyn! That's all the beds you got tonight? Just Brooklyn! Shit!!" they say.

"Yes, that's the only place there are beds tonight."

"Shit. I ain't going to no fucking Brooklyn! You sure that's it? Nothing in Midtown, or maybe the Wall Street area?"

"No. That's it. All we have is the shelter in Bedford Stuyvesant," I say.

"Fuck, if that's all you got, I'm leaving. I gotta be in Manhattan, man. Maybe I'll come back tomorrow night."

And they get up and leave, back to the streets or park or wherever.

I've learned that homeless people prefer to be in Manhattan, just like everybody else. At first I was indignant—these people are *choosy* about where they're going to stay? But I thought about it and realized that the sources of their livelihood, such as they are, are far more lucrative in Manhattan. Panhandling goes much better in Times Square than in Far Rockaway. The men tell me that if you do it respectfully and look decrepit enough—but not so decrepit as to scare people—you can make between twenty and eighty dollars an hour panhandling in a prime location in Midtown. They may be mentally ill, but they're usually not crazy: it's to Manhattan that the voices tell them to go, and not, for example, to Staten Island.

"So, why did you come to New York . . . that is, Manhattan?" I almost always ask the people in the black chair.

Some of the answers I've heard over the years:

"Because Jesus told me to."

"Because someone was trying to kill me in Las Vegas."

"Because where I was staying they only let you stay in chairs, and I want a bed."

"Because when I got out of prison in Baltimore I read that Giuliani had brought the crime rate down so I decided to return to New York."

"Because this is where the bus brought me."

"Because I can get better health insurance here than in Puerto Rico."

"Because I can't find my way home. I left my house on Walters Street in the Bronx ten years ago and I can't find my way back."

"Because I'm John the Baptist—a truth serum given to me at Trenton State Hospital in 1969 proves it—and can you get me a bed near the St. John the Divine Cathedral because I have to go there and tell them I've arrived."

"Who said I was in New York?"

"Because when I was working on the chicken farm in Georgia last week, a voice told me to come here."

"Because I always wanted to see the Empire State Building."

"Because the people here are less crappy than they are in Florida."

"To compete in a karate championship."

"Because I want to open a blacksmith shop in Queens."

"Because my so-called best friend stole everything I had."

"Because I always wanted to go where no one would find me."

❧ ❧ ❧

But even among the travelers there are the prodigious and ceaseless wanderers, those who are committed to motion as a way of life. Traveling around America—which in this case means visiting one shelter and soup kitchen and church basement and subway station and bus depot and abandoned building after another—is their profession. In the warmer weather, and even in the colder weather, a lot of them camp out, whether it is in Central Park, the woods of upstate New York, or the beaches of California. It doesn't seem to matter really where they are, as long as they can move away from it quickly. A lot of them are actually offered permanent or semipermanent lodging—halfway houses, community residences, and the like—and they invariably turn them down, preferring to move on to the next city. Their destinations are much like those featured in travel advertisements: New Orleans, Las Vegas, L.A., Hawaii, and New York.

There is a specific look to the professional travelers, instantly identifiable—there is almost invariably a certain healthy and woodsy glow about them, no matter how high or drunk or crazy they are. They tend to have long straggly beards and wild eyes and dusty backpacks and sleeping bags. In the summer they wear as little as possible and have dark tans, and their hair gets blond from the sun; in the winter they wear layers of sweaters and have rosy cheeks. They are usually lean. A few of them, self-consciously or not, adopt the romantic trappings of the old hoboes. One night a man plaintively played a harmonica in the waiting room, entertaining his fellow wayfarers. Once I walked past Central Park and saw a group of hoboes sitting around and roasting marshmallows at a campfire, like something out of *The Treasure of the Sierra Madre*. The parallel universe of Central Park West and its fabulously expensive French restaurants, celebrity apartment houses, and endless plush medical—typically psychiatrists'—offices was just thirty feet away.

The shelter staff came to me one night, exasperated, saying there was a white guy somewhere in the building who had been eluding them for hours. The shelter workers had been trying to get his photograph and fingerprints—both required to enter the shelter—but this person, whoever he was, had been stealthily moving from chair to chair and room to room all night long. In other words, he was a traveler even within the confines of the shelter.

"Where is he now?" I asked the security officer.

"In the bathroom—we think," he said, and led me there.

The bathroom was a predictably dingy, rank affair, distinguished only by the curious fact that the dividers between the stalls were made of marble, with beautiful gray swirling patterns in it. On the marble was written, in magic marker and in huge letters, "Bums never have a nice day," and "Suck my homeless dick." The man sitting on the toilet had tousled reddish blond hair—lots of it—and a thick beard. He was rocking back and forth on the toilet, with his pants on. He looked, I thought, like a psychotic Viking.

"Excuse me," I said, "would you mind going to have your photograph taken in the screening room? And when you're done, would you mind coming to my office down the hall?"

"Oh yeah, sure, sure, sure," he replied.

I left there as quickly as possible, thinking that I had done my job for the night and that I would never see him again. But when I turned around a moment later, back in the office, the Viking was sitting quietly in the black chair next to me.

"What's your name?" I said.

"Leif," he said. It sounded Nordic or Danish, confirming my Viking theory. He probably would have been a great Viking, I thought; a few thousand years ago his wildness would have served him well. As I was contemplating this, he began doing a kind of dance in the chair—arms and legs and hands and head bouncing away, all of them flowing to different beats—and embarked on a rushed monologue:

"In case you wanted to know, I'm Norwegian, Ukrainian, Swedish, Danish, Irish," he began. "I've lived in Florida, Hawaii, Alaska, Oklahoma, all over Canada, and Cheyenne, Wyoming, but mainly I grew up in South Jersey. The malls suck there, you know? I slept under a car last night. I was in jail for a rape I didn't commit of my half sister. What else do you need to know?"

"Have you been in the shelter system before?" I asked.

He looked directly at me. "I need help. I need help! No one's helping me . . . After I got out of detox," he said, and as he said it I noticed for the first time that his breath stank of liquor, "I didn't have nowhere to go. That's why I'm here. But not for long. Thinking of going back to Cheyenne. That was my favorite place. Happy there. That's where I got convicted of the rape I didn't commit of my half sister"—I noticed he used the exact same phrasing to describe the alleged crime—"and I want to clear my record. Clear my name!"

"Have you been in the hospital recently?" I said.

"I have very bad nerves," he said, not exactly to me but, it seemed, to something beyond me—a general statement to or about the world. "VERY BAD NERVES," he added for emphasis. "You know who helped me! The nuns helped me. The nuns were fucking AWESOME!" he shouted to the ceiling, and then smiled broadly.

"Do you take any medications?" I said.

"I brought it all on myself," he said. "Nobody's fault but mine." He stood up and produced from his pockets a series of smudged and torn-up hospital papers. The papers said that he had been in a hospital in Maine and before that a detox in Providence and before that a psychiatric hospital in Kansas and before that a rehab in Oregon, and that he had severe diabetes, a seizure disorder, and bipolar disorder. The medical diagnoses surprised me, in a way: he had that healthy look of the travelers, that unworried and rural look that made it seem that at a moment's notice he could set off on a fifty-mile hike in the woods.

Suddenly he lurched forward in the chair and thirty syringes fell to the floor. They seemed to have fallen out of his red sweatshirt, but from where exactly, I couldn't tell. He picked up the syringes, one after the other, and stuffed them into his pockets and what seemed like a pouch in his sweatshirt. As he picked up the needles, he kept on talking, not stopping for a second, about nuns, disputed rapes, Cheyenne, and bad malls in New Jersey. At one point he took out a thick wad of bills, again from some mysterious place on his person. "See this!" he said, waving the money right up to my face. "It's chump change, and it means nothing," he said, and immediately went back to picking up syringes. Finally he was done, and I got him to sit down again.

"When was the last time you took your meds?" I said.

"The physical shit is nothing. It's a test, a test! I wish I woulda died after the seizure, I wish I woulda never woken up. Then I wouldn't have to deal with the HASSLE. The physical shit is nothing. It's a test by Jesus Christ, a test by God to see how much you can take. The only thing, man, is I gotta keep moving. Death is being static, dude."

I was about to ask him more about tests by Jesus Christ and hassles and nuns, because I liked him and was interested, when he jumped again—as if electrically shocked by something in the chair—and ran out of the room. By the time I got out into the hallway, he was gone. A few syringes had fallen out of his pocket and were bouncing on the shiny floor of the shelter. Fortuitously, the security officer hadn't been at his post, and Leif, the psychotic Viking, the adventurer, was able to leave undetected, free to reenter his world.

There's another section of our Department of Mental Health–approved forms regarding the outcome of the services we provide. At the conclusion of each visit, we're supposed to check off "Accepts Assessment" in the case of a successful result, and "Left Shelter" in the case of an unsuccessful one. For Leif, I clicked "Left Shelter" and then sat in the quiet of my office reflecting on the natural storm I had just encountered. For a few minutes I worried about Leif and where he was, but then I stopped. I realized I didn't feel bad at all about his departure. I didn't know what provoked the electrical shock that made him bolt, but I did know that he'd be better off out there, journeying to his mental Wyoming.

He'll be happier out there, I thought. He'll be happier out there, in America. On the computer, I clicked "Accepts Assessment."

⚬ ⚬ ⚬

Here at the shelter, the Vietnam War continues to be fought on a nightly basis.

Vietnam vets sit in the black chair at alarming rates. Almost every night, it seems, we get someone who was, and perhaps still is, in Vietnam. Or at least some version of Vietnam.

He was well over six feet, probably closer to six and a half. He was muscular and lean, even in his depleted state. It was clear, from the vapor that rose from his breath and the redness of his eyes and an interesting kind of melted quality of his black flesh, that he was a deeply committed alcoholic. As he sat quietly in the black chair, I could sense the ranginess and the sheer physical power of his limbs. His forehead was sweating, and the sweat seemed to smell of pure alcohol. He conveyed an ineffable and monstrous sadness. He appeared, as he sat in front of me, to have been scorched by some unspeakable horror.

"Did you have something to drink tonight?" I said.

"I have something to drink every night," he replied, with an aggrieved expression of enormous disdain.

I was working that night with a bookish and rather earnest social worker. "Why do you drink?" Mark asked the man.

"why?" Another look of infinite disdain, this time directed toward Mark.

"Why do I drink? Why do I drink?" he said, his anger seeming to rise within him. Why wouldn't I drink?, he seemed to be thinking. "I drink to forget. I drink to forget." And then he said it for a third time, as if to fully cement it in his mind. "I drink to forget."

"To forget what?" Mark said.

"Vietnam, man. I drink to forget Vietnam," he said.

"And what about Vietnam in particular?" Mark said.

"What in particular?" he said. The man in the black chair looked toward me, as if appealing for help. The look on his face, a mixture of anger and consternation, said that of all the stupid questions he had been asked by all the stupid social workers in his entire life, this was by far the stupidest. I was about to intervene, to say he really didn't need to answer, when he spat out, in a torrent of words: "I was a good soldier. A fucking good soldier. A fucking warrior. Everything they told me to do, I did it. I was real good at following orders. They told me drop something, I dropped it. They told me to pick something up, I picked it up. They told me to kill people, I killed people. I was very, very good at it. I think I killed a lot of people. I don't know how many—maybe hundreds, maybe more. I don't know. It was hard to tell in Vietnam what the hell was going on. All I know is I killed and killed and killed. I see pictures of it in my head. Bodies and shit. I drink to forget that, see?"

Done with his speech, the Warrior appeared to be suddenly spent. He seemed to enter some other, less present state of being, his eyes taking on a faraway look.

Indeed, I could imagine the Warrior being an excellent killer. I saw visions of him charging through jungles, firing manically away, a brilliant killing machine. I saw him in swamps and battlefields, with bombs and grenades, with lots and lots of dead people left in his wake.

"Did you ever think of . . . you know . . . like joining a peer group of any kind?" Mark said.

"A what?" said the Warrior. His look of outrage returned.

"You know, like a peer group for Vietnam vets who have gone through the same thing and have addiction issues?"

The Warrior again appealed to me for help. A peer group, whatever that was, seemed to be much worse than anything he'd encountered in Vietnam.

"Nope, never thought of that," he said. "I really just came here for a bed. It's cold outside, you know?"

I nodded.

"I just want a fucking bed," he said.

I'm supposed to recommend further psychiatric assessment and treatment for those clients who I think would benefit from it. I've learned to recommend that only if the client is interested in or able to change. I wrote on my form "Client is capable of negotiating shelter system," which is what I put when I have no recommendations.

"Do you mind giving me your V.A. card?" I asked the Warrior. He handed it to me, and I quickly wrote down his date of birth and service number for the chart.

"Any more questions for us?" I said, realizing that there had been none so far.

"Nope."

"Okay, you can go back to the waiting room. The bus will be here in a few hours to take you to the shelter in Brooklyn."

"Okay," he said and left. He looked momentarily happy, realizing the questions were over.

Later that night I entered the Warrior's personal data into the computer. His birth date on the V.A. card was 11-3-55.

November 3, 1955.

"Hold on," I said, turning to Mark. "This guy couldn't have been in Vietnam. He would have been what . . . seventeen . . . when the war ended."

"Yeah?" Mark said.

"There's no way he was there. He was underage, under eighteen, in 1972."

"You mean he was making all that stuff up?"

"I guess," I said. "He must have been. Jesus Christ."

I did the math again. Yeah, seventeen. It wouldn't have been possible.

I was angry. I really wanted to see him as a Warrior. I sort of liked those images of him running through the jungle, fighting for democracy or American imperialism, or whatever. If he were a Warrior, then he had the right to drink all he wanted. If he wasn't . . .

"Who knows," I said.

"No wonder he didn't want to go to any support groups," Mark said.

"Who fucking knows," I said.

⚓ ⚓ ⚓

Last January I was asked by the security staff to go to the entrance of the shelter to assess a problem case, a guy in a wheelchair. Security wouldn't let him into the building because he didn't have papers to prove that he was medically cleared to enter the shelter system. When I saw the guy sitting in the strangely ornate entry foyer (it has marble floors and a hand-painted ceiling), I knew why they called me. He was in a wheelchair, had no arms and no legs, and wore a loose cotton hospital gown that was open to the waist, revealing a still-oozing stomach wound. He was distressingly thin, had black curly hair, and looked Italian. A teddy bear was in his lap. A sparkly heart-shaped balloon, with the words "I LOVE YOU" printed on it in expansive letters, was attached by a string to the back of his wheelchair. "I'm Richie Vecchio," he said, smiling at me. He appeared to be in no distress.

I wheeled him down the dark hall to the waiting room. The security guards looked at us dubiously—all they knew was that he wasn't authorized to come in. I looked closely at his hospital bracelet. It indicated that he had been an inpatient at Bellevue for the last four months.

"What unit?" I said.

"Medical," Richie said. "I was in an accident," he said happily.

I told him that they wouldn't let him into the shelter unless he got a form from a doctor stating that he was medically stable.

"You better go back to the hospital. Then you can come back here," I said.

"Oh, I'm not going back there," he said. "I've been there for four months."

As a legal matter, I explained, they weren't going to let him in the shelter.

"Oh, that's okay," he said, reassuring me. "I'm just happy to be out of the hospital."

"Did you sign yourself out?" I asked.

"Yup," he said with satisfaction.

"But where will you go?"

"Oh, I'll figure something out," he said.

I started in on the legalese I've been trained with: "It is of course your right to leave the hospital, but I strongly urge you . . . ," when he interrupted me.

"It's all right, man, I'm just happy to be free," Richie said. "But I was wondering, do you think you could let me stay in the building long enough so I could recharge my wheelchair? The batteries don't last long in the cold."

He had spotted the electrical outlet in the corner. He pushed his chin down into his chest and engaged a button on a metal plate that lay on his collarbone. The wheelchair whirred forward.

"See the cord in the back? Could you plug it in?" he said. "It takes about forty-five minutes to charge up." I plugged in the cord.

"Is your wound okay?"

"Jeez," he observed, looking down at it for the first time. "I guess it is oozing a little."

"What happened to you anyway?" I said.

"Lost my limbs in a motorcycle accident. My fault," he said. "I'm an addict. Heroin, coke, everything. Now I'm just on methadone, and a ton of medications." It was as if he were talking about varieties of ice cream.

He directed me to a pouch on the back of his wheelchair. In it was a hospital paper that said he had hepatitis and HIV. There were about fifteen bottles of medications in there.

"Are you sure you don't want to go back to the hospital?"

"No way!" he said almost violently. "Four months is enough. They won't take me back anyway."

"Let me see if I can find anything for you," I said.

There are, in New York City, strange entities called drop-in centers. They are intended to work as adjuncts to the city shelter system. They are meant, by design, to assist those who aren't medically cleared or deemed "appropriate" for the regular system. That is, they serve those poor souls who have been rejected by the shelter system. The drop-in centers provide only the most minimal "shelter": usually they are a couple of basement rooms in a church. Contractually they are not allowed to provide beds. The clients of the drop-in centers sit on chairs all night long.

I called the four drop-in centers in Manhattan. I made my usual mistake, which is to ask if they have beds.

"You mean *chairs*," said an annoyed voice at the first drop-in center.

"Yes, chairs," I said.

"No chairs," the voice said, and hung up the phone.

I called the next drop-in center. "Do you have any . . . er . . . slots?"

"You mean *chairs*," said the voice. "No, didn't you notice? It's cold outside. No chairs." Click.

No chairs were to be had at the other drop-in centers either.

When I returned to the waiting room there were three more clients waiting. Normally the guys in the waiting room never talk to one another, instead sitting silently with their heads down, avoiding eye contact at all costs. But these three were all talking to Richie. One was sharing his sandwich with him, and another was reading him a story from the newspaper.

"I'm sorry, I couldn't find anything for you. Do you have any money?" I said.

"One hundred and thirty dollars," said Richie, precisely.

The last resort for shelter that night was the Bowery flophouses. Usually they charge ten dollars a night for a room with walls made of chicken wire. I called the usual places: The Palace, The Rio, The Sunshine. None of them had beds. "It's cold outside," the voices on the other end of the line said. My last call was to the YMCA, ten blocks away.

"We have a bed, but you gotta get here quick," said the attendant.

"How much?"

"Sixty-five dollars a night." In New York, even the Ys are expensive.

"Oh, that's fine," Richie said, after I told him about the Y. "I'll go there."

"But you only have enough for two nights."

"It's okay. Don't worry, man. I'll figure something out."

He depressed his chin and engaged the button. He rolled out of the waiting room. "See you guys later. Thanks a lot," he said, nodding to his instant friends.

We left the shelter. Smoke or steam or whatever it is that emanates from the city's innards was billowing up through an open manhole to the surface of First Avenue. The wind had picked up. It must have been twenty degrees outside. Richie told me he had a jacket in his pouch, and I put it on him. It wasn't much more than a windbreaker. All he had on underneath was the cotton hospital gown. I pointed him in the direction of the McBurney YMCA.

"Do you think the wheelchair will make it?"

"Probably. We'll see. It looks like it's downhill," he said, laughing. He headed out into the street.

Then he stopped and shouted back to me. "See ya later! Thanks a lot, man. Thanks a lot, Charlie, I mean it. I really appreciate everything you've done for me. You're a great social worker or doctor, or whatever you are."

He whirred across First Avenue, almost getting hit by a bus. He whirred unsteadily down one side of the avenue, in the few feet between the parked cars and the oncoming traffic. The last I saw of him was the back of his wheelchair, the heart-shaped balloon bouncing in the wind, as he cut through a cloud of steam coming out of the street.

For some reason, watching that last image of Richie heading to oblivion, I thought suddenly of Henry. Sure, Henry was in a lot of pain, but he had his arms and legs, and he didn't have hepatitis or AIDS or a methadone addiction or an oozing stomach wound. He had intelligence and money and a family that loved him—albeit in a difficult way—and he had his physical health, and he could have fucking survived, I thought. I was sure of it now, he could have made it. Dammit, Henry, I thought, on the corner of East 29th Street and First Avenue. You had everything to live for.

᛭ ᛭ ᛭

I've worked a lot of holidays at Bellevue: Independence Day, Thanksgiving, Christmas, Labor Day. Homelessness doesn't stop on holidays, but it does slow down. I've noticed that there aren't too many applicants for shelter on the holidays. I think the clients know it's a little tough to be in a homeless shelter on Christmas, and they stay away.

I watched the millennium come in at the shelter, saw the digital clock turn to 12:00:01 a.m., 2000. Here at the shelter, nothing changed. No one celebrated. Homelessness in the new millennium seemed to be just about the same as it was in the last one.

But the holiday I'll always remember was last July 4th. The shelter, about fifty yards from the East River, is a great spot to watch the fireworks from. The explosives are set off in barges in the middle of the river. The city closes down FDR Drive for the night, and the crowds arrive two or three hours before the display to get a good view. At Bellevue, we have the same view all to ourselves.

Last year I started watching the fireworks from the shelter waiting room. There was nobody in the room but me, and I looked down on the vast and noisy crowds on the streets. The crowd had swelled to about fifty yards thick, packed in behind police barricades. I watched the psychedelic explosions for half an hour and then went back to my office.

From my office window I could see the massive second wing of the building. About a hundred windows in all faced me across the garbage-strewn courtyard. As the fireworks continued, I noticed that there were some faces peering out of some of the windows. At first it was too dark to see clearly, but as the side of the building lit up for a few seconds in pink or green or purple after the more-impressive explosions, I could see that there were dozens and dozens of faces—almost all of them black—looking out of the windows. It was like a delayed strobe: every twenty seconds or so, I could see those peering heads, each time lit with a different color. As I stared longer, and my eyes adjusted to the strobe, I could read the expressions on the faces. They all had the same expression, and it was an odd look, one that I'd never seen before at the shelter, where most people try to be as numb as possible. It was an expression of shy longing, a wish to be a part of something that was unavailable to them. America, it seemed, was a party they could observe but not attend. In a moment, I realized how strangely and cruelly exhilarating, how terribly and punishingly great, it was to work at the shelter.

And across the courtyard, there was still that longing on those faces. They wanted to merge into those streaming lights over Brooklyn. All of them, I thought, every single one of the residents of the black chair—Leif, the Warrior, Richie, Henry—they all wanted to embrace the green light. All of them had songs they sang, songs in the midst of despair—songs about mythical places like Cheyenne and Vietnam and about bobbing red balloons . . . there is something much greater out there somewhere . . . and perhaps somehow, some way, someday . . . .

⋄ ⋄ ⋄

When I drive home after leaving the Bellevue shelter at midnight, my thirteen-hour circuit at homeless shelters done for the day, I usually feel pretty good. I feel like I've accomplished something, given something, perhaps, to the people in Manhattan who have schizophrenia. I've taken my OCD and done something constructive with it. Often as I drive through the trafficless streets of the city at midnight, I feel light, elevated, joyous. Yes, joyous. I think it's an elation that goes beyond the Prozac coursing through my veins. On my way home I stop at the all-night gas station on the highway near the George Washington Bridge and fill up my car. As the gas flows through the nozzle into the tank, sometimes I see myself somersaulting in the air and see myself spinning up into the night sky. I see myself go farther and farther up. Eventually I am way above New York, attached to earth only by the hose from the gas pump, which has magically reeled out to be a mile long. I look down at the city below me, with its millions of blinking lights. Manhattan looks like a toy, a miniature model of a real city. I dance and spin for a while up in the atmosphere, where, I notice, it has just started to snow. Small flakes of white fall on my black leather jacket. I do one more spin and then the gas pump hose retracts and I am pulled gently back to Route 4 in New Jersey. When I hit the earth my tank is full.

"Have a good night," the attendant says to me after I pay him.

"I will," I say emphatically.

Sometimes, horribly, I think this: I am glad Henry died, and I am glad I have OCD. It has allowed me to do this work. I am a more troubled but a more effective person as a result of OCD. Without this work, I would be worthless and boring. OCD and Henry saved me from being ordinary.

nine

The Fort

I *do* love the work.

When I was a graduate student I had a twenty-hour-a-week job working as an assistant editor and researcher at a kind of a think tank, a media studies center in the journalism school. I liked the job well enough, but every day at about 4 p.m. I would become fearsomely depressed. It was partly the late afternoon blahs, but mainly it was this: I wondered what I'd been doing all day. In that late afternoon light, my work seemed utterly empty, manipulating words and symbols for no apparent reason or effect.

I never feel that way at the shelter. Whatever its shortcomings, which are primarily financial, it is an extraordinary place to work. (Regarding the poor pay: from time to time I have picked up extra work—catering at an auction house, tutoring high school students—and it is a matter of record that baking and selling brownies or correcting a fifteen-year-old's algebra homework pays two to three times better than long hours working with the homeless mentally ill.) But I don't mind my thirteen-hour days—the day shift at the shelter in the former armory uptown, which we call "the Fort," and the night shift at Bellevue. The work is so obviously rewarding, and so obviously not boring.

Much of the day is filled with humor, collegiality, and great appreciation for what the staff does. (The clients thank us all day long for our work.) Many of the clients are obviously impaired and suffering, but I wouldn't describe the place as anguished or tragic. It doesn't *feel* tragic on a moment-to-moment basis. I'm not sure why this is, exactly. Perhaps it occupies a space beyond tragedy—where there is nothing left to lose, which is oddly peaceful—or maybe it's that none of us can sustain permanent anguish, but it is a place of frequent jokes and laughter.

There is a structure to the day—a morning community meeting, various group meetings (on medications, on the signs of mental illness, on substance abuse, etc.), meetings with case managers, and outings in the afternoon and evening to movies and sometimes even concerts and Broadway plays, courtesy of a wonderful organization that gives free tickets to people with disabilities. But the structure is only the surface. What makes the job interesting is that it does not yield to predictability.

It is pointless to describe a typical day at the Fort. I can only describe a typical *beginning* to the day, which involves walking through a large metal detector and going upstairs into the two dingy rooms of the shelter's psychiatric clinic. On the way I walk past the twelve dorm rooms that house a total of two hundred men, each having a psychotic diagnosis, and I walk past the medical clinic, the dining room, a TV room, two bathrooms, and, most popular of all, a smoke room. The smoke room is painted every three months by the shelter staff, but no matter: within a few weeks the walls return to the smudgy gray color they had been before. It is the only aspect of the Fort that feels awful. Men slump over tables, trying to sleep, trying to forget, while the others smoke and stare at the walls. Unless there is a card game, no one talks. Fifty men look out at nothing, each in a different direction.

In the clinic, I sit at my desk—used, beat-up furniture, discarded from some office—and read the "Incident Log" from the night before. It might describe someone smoking crack in the dorms, someone else having a personal dialogue with Jesus, and a third waking up half the floor in the middle of the night by reciting his manic poetry. After that, we open the doors to the clinic, the clients come in for coffee and the morning meeting, and then there is no longer any script.

◦❖ ◦❖ ◦❖

"Don't you get tired of it?" my mother once asked, in the safety and comfort of my parent's suburban home, as I told her about the Fort.

"No," I said, automatically. "Well, a little. It can be rough. But I feel I'm involved in trying to make things sane, so in a curious way, it feels orderly. It feels 'not crazy,'" I offered. "And there are funny moments, too. A lot of times it's like one big happy family."

My mother looked across at me, disbelieving.

⌐ ⌐ ⌐

"Is Robert there?" said the voice on the other end of the phone.

Robert Foster was my boss, the psychiatrist in charge of the shelter.

"No, he's not," I said.

"Could you leave him a message? Tell him that it's his host from the casino, and I'm just passing on my regards. My beeper number is 230–1568; please pass it on to Mr. Wellington and tell him he can call at any time, at his convenience."

"Mr. Wellington?" I said.

"Yes, Mr. Robert Wellington," said the voice. "And please give Mr. Wellington my best regards."

Robert Wellington was a Fort resident, known for his forays — when manic — to Atlantic City for "a little action," as he put it, of the gambling and female variety.

I didn't bother to pass on the message.

A week later, I got another phone call.

"Is Mr. Robert Wellington available? This is Ricky Salazar, his host at the casino. I wanted again to pass on my beeper number, and to pass on my best regards."

This time I passed on the message. I found Robert in the smoke room, in one of Dante's circles of hell. Robert was holding court over a game of cards.

"They like you down there in Atlantic City?" I said.

Robert smiled. He was a huge man, six feet four, probably 260 pounds, with a fine, broad smile and a deep, knowing laugh. Like virtually all the residents of the Fort he wore a baseball cap and other sports-related gear, like a football team jersey (among other reasons, so as to better blend in with others on the street and in the subway). "Oh yeah, they like me," he said. "I just won $30,000 down there the other week, and I tipped the guy pretty good. I was feeling no pain," Robert said, laughing a little too loudly.

"I see," I said. Of course I didn't believe him. You learned not to believe half of what you heard.

A few days later, Robert approached me and pulled me into a quiet corner, which is hard to find at the Fort.

"Charlie, do me a favor," he said conspiratorially. "Can you make a copy of this check? I want a copy of it in the files in case I lose it." He held a check for $30,000 from an Atlantic City casino in his hand. "I don't want to cash it or nothing 'cause I don't want to fuck up my benefits."

Robert was unusual among residents of the Fort in that he accepted his diagnosis, and was very careful to maintain his Medicaid insurance, on which we depended to get his medications. He was right: if he cashed that check, his benefits would be terminated. If he had more than $2,000 in the bank, according to Social Security rules, his benefits—by virtue of the noxious web of computers and wires that connects public entitlements to bank accounts and other types of supposedly private files—would be instantly cut off.

"I'm holding on to it until I'm ready to start my business up again," he said, pointing to his head in a vague indication that stuff up there still needed to be straightened out. Robert had been a taxi driver before he got sick, and his dream was to start a private limousine service. I returned the check to him. He put it back in his flimsy wallet and laughed that deep bull laugh.

I laughed too. It's stuff like that that makes me want to put in my daily thirteen-hour quota at homeless shelters.

᠅ ᠅ ᠅

But I must confess—I like the crises. The crises are rare, but they happen. I don't like violence, which is *exceedingly* rare, but I like the excitement that the prospect of violence brings. I find it exhilarating to help de-escalate crisis situations, and it seems I've developed an ability to slow down when things get tense. And I know exactly where these skills come from—from my long, hard-won experience with taming the violent threats of my own OCD.

᠅ ᠅ ᠅

At the Fort, we order a lot of pizza.

One of the clients caught on one day. "I know what ordering pizza is," he said to one of the case managers. "That's when you think one of us is going to go off, and you say to the other staff that you're ordering pizza but what you're actually doing is calling 911 for them to take us away."

"No, no," said the case manager. "It's when we're really hungry, and we want to get something to eat."

The police show up really quickly after you call for pizza. And usually in force—four or five of them. As soon as you mention on the phone that the person in question is a psychiatric patient—or an "EDP" (emotionally disturbed person) in cop speak—you get the sense that they take it pretty seriously.

When Curtis mentioned casually in the morning community meeting that he was thinking of murdering his boyfriend later that day (because he thought he was cheating on him), I calmly walked to my desk and ordered the pizza. While we were waiting for the police to show up, I asked Curtis to talk to me at my desk. He said he was "just fucking with us" about his friend. And he probably was just messing around, but then again Curtis had only been at the shelter for a few days after leaving prison for stabbing someone.

I'm never sure whether to inform the clients that I've called the police. I hate feeling like a snitch, but if you tell them, there's a good chance they'll flee. In this case I waited until I knew that the cops had entered the building before I told Curtis.

He said, "I can't fucking believe it. I was just joking. I can't fucking believe you did that."

Eight cops showed up. After Curtis screamed at them, they formed a semicircle and backed him into a corner. When he refused to comply, they pinned his arms against the wall and applied handcuffs. With a phalanx of policemen encircling him, he was marched out of the day room. Walking past me, Curtis gave me a look to burn my soul. I followed the impromptu parade as Curtis and the police exited the shelter and walked diagonally across the street to the emergency room. I had written a note for the staff at the psychiatric emergency room explaining what had occurred, and also that Curtis had AIDS, a crack addiction, and by his report forty psychiatric hospitalizations. (He was only twenty-three—I think he exaggerated.) In the ER Curtis said to me, under his breath, "I want to kill you, motherfucker."

To the surprise of none of us, Curtis was released two days later.

When he returned to the shelter the next week—he took a few days after the hospitalization to stay with his boyfriend—I met with him again. I was nervous and asked a security guard to sit in with us. But now Curtis was calm and respectful. He liked me now. It seemed I was worthy of respect, almost macho, because I'd taken a stand. We were now man to man, *hombre a hombre*. For the next two weeks, until he moved into housing for people with AIDS, Curtis and I got along just fine. He took to greeting me warmly like we were old pals, and calling me "Mr. Barber."

⋄ ⋄ ⋄

The report, written in the log from the previous night, said that Etienne had been overheard in the bathroom talking about assassinating the president.

Neither Dr. Mercado, one of the psychiatrists, nor I had ever seen Etienne, although we had read about him in the night logs. One of the case managers had worked at the Fort for six years and had never laid eyes on Etienne. This was because Etienne spent all his time in the bathroom on the ground floor. He was the shelter's own Boo Radley.

It was rumored that Etienne had never set foot outside the shelter in the six years he'd been there. He was in the bathroom all day, briefly in the dining room for meals, and slept in his dorm room, if he didn't return to the bathroom at night. He never caused any problems in the bathroom—he just was there—but in the last week we had gotten some complaints from other residents that Etienne had approached them "inappropriately." He had been talking to people as they were showering, mumbling things about President Bush. I knew from his chart that he thought he was a member of the Bush family and believed he had direct communication with the White House, but only when he was in the bathroom.

Dr. Mercado and I walked through the long, dingy corridors to the residents' bathroom. We peered into the bathroom shared by two hundred men—a not-so-large grayish moist and dingy room with six stalls and an adjoining shower room—but it was empty.

We went into the cafeteria. There alone on a bench sat a composed, almost fresh-looking man (how could he look so fresh after spending all his time in that grungy bathroom?), with a cup of coffee in front of him. His snow-white beard contrasted brilliantly with his dark skin.

"Mr. DeClaire?" I said. Etienne nodded.

We all shook hands. The palm of his hand, I remember thinking, was exceptionally smooth. I'm not sure why, but I expected something rougher.

"Is there anything that we can help you with today?" I asked.

"No, no, everything is fine." He spoke with a thick Haitian accent.

"Do you have any concerns, about the bathroom or President Bush?" Dr. Mercado said.

"No, no, everything is fine," he said.

"We'd like to see you in our program. We have coffee and bagels in the morning, and then we have groups, and a lot of medical services. Why don't you come by and see us some time?"

"No, no, fine," he said.

We spoke some more, about nothing in particular.

"Are you having thoughts of hurting anyone?" Dr. Mercado said.

"No, of course not."

We tried to ask him again, in various ways, if there was anything we could do, anything he had concerns about, encouraging him to come to our program. He refused all help and was as composed as could be.

Dr. Mercado and I walked back upstairs. "He seemed pretty calm," I said.

"Yeah," Mercado said.

"Do you think we can hospitalize him?" I said.

"I don't think we have any grounds to," Mercado said. "And besides, how's he going to kill President Bush if he never leaves the shelter?"

◆ ◆ ◆

John was my first murderer.

At my desk in the Fort, John, a sad-eyed and earnest Chinese-American man, told me in halting and dismayed tones that he had killed his brother. John had been ten years old, and his brother eighteen, when John pushed him in front of a train. John told me he'd kept it a secret for twenty-five years, and I was only the second person he'd told since informing a psychiatrist a month ago.

I thought John had excellent reason to push him. His older brother had been sexually abusing him as far back as he could remember. On the night of his death, his brother, who happened to be standing at the edge of the tracks, had called John over, presumably to touch him. Without thinking much about it—or so he told me—John charged him and pushed him as an oncoming train hurtled by. It all took a matter of seconds. He heard his brother's echoing cry as he was hit. John then went to his family's apartment and told his mother that his brother had been drunk and had been killed in an accident on the tracks. Everybody believed his story, including the police. There was no suspicion of foul play. But every night John saw his dead brother—appearing as a boy, about the same age as John was when the murder occurred—standing over him at the edge of the bed, smiling. John would try to talk to him, but the dead brother would just stand there, smiling and hovering. After each night's apparition, John couldn't get back to sleep. Dark circles under his eyes, which seemed to be a permanent part of his face, attested to his story.

The confession seemed to bring John some relief. He was terribly concerned that we would report him to the police, and when we did not, he visibly relaxed. The nightly vision of his brother did not completely disappear, but it seemed to dissipate. John had come to us after being in prison for three years for drug dealing, and he had a history in prison of fighting. But at the Fort he was one of our most placid and conscientious clients: he showed up at the clinic daily, took his medications, attended group therapy, met with his psychiatrist, stayed clean of substances, and never showed a hint of aggression. After a couple of months, he moved out, happily it seemed to me, to live with his girlfriend.

I found it exhilarating. It was exhilarating that people like John entrusted me with their stories, and it was exhilarating to observe him appear to get better. I felt like I was doing something with my life, which was an unaccustomed, somewhat odd, and deeply pleasurable sensation.

⚬ ⚬ ⚬

But when the ultimate crisis came, the response wasn't at all what I expected.

On the morning of September 11, 2001, I was unable to get into

Manhattan because of the attack on the World Trade towers. Laura and I spent the day at home, listening to the fighter jets circle in the skies above our house, smelling the encroaching smoke emanating from the colossal fires in lower Manhattan, seventeen miles away, and watching the reports on television. Later in the day, when the telephone circuits were no longer overloaded, Laura and I called family and friends and tried to be as quiet and domestic as we could in the face of the obliteration that had just occurred. It was hard, though, not to think of those hundreds of people pitching themselves out of the towers.

I wasn't able to get into Manhattan until two days later. It took me hours to drive to the Fort, but I very much wanted to be there. I felt a responsibility to be at the shelter to assist or simply be present during what must surely be a period of crisis for many of the residents. I drove across the George Washington Bridge to find a New York City that was almost unrecognizable from the one I had left seventy-two hours before. In addition to the huge smoldering fire obscuring the southern end of the island, there was the constant drone of sirens and car alarms, and more emergency vehicles on the roads than civilian ones. The streets and sidewalks were largely empty, and those people who were out were quiet and taut and angry-looking. There was no laughter, no flow of conversation, not even the usual New York sounds of car horns and people yelling at each other in traffic. American flags were everywhere—on cars, on lapel buttons, on the top of apartment buildings. On a telephone booth were the words KILL ALL ARABS. So, I thought, this is what it feels like to be a city at war. Imagining how crazy things were going to be at the shelter, I felt even more nervous than I had been driving into the city.

I ran the community meeting that morning. Normally we check in with the clients, go through the upcoming day's schedule (the various activities and therapeutic groups), and then have an open discussion. I looked around the room at the thirty clients there, faces I knew well. They looked oddly composed, fresh, almost ebullient. I'd hardly ever seen them looking so good. Everything proceeded as it always did. Nobody mentioned recent events, like the fact that a part of the city had recently disappeared.

When we came to the open discussion part of the meeting, I asked, "Does anyone have concerns they want to bring up?"

Someone raised their hand and complained about the hot water in the showers. A fairly long discussion ensued about how best to raise this issue with the building manager.

Then someone else asked when his stipend check would be available.

"What about the World Trade Center attacks," I said. "Any thoughts on that?" That's what I said, but what I was thinking was: are you all so selfish and self-absorbed that you don't care or are not aware that thousands and thousands of New Yorkers died brutally the other day a few miles from here, and that the next ten years of our lives will be indelibly linked to this event, or is it all about the fucking hot water and the disability checks?

"Oh, no, we already talked about that yesterday," said one of the clients, rather complacently. "We already discussed it."

And at that they all got up to end the meeting, exuding that same odd ebullience and evenness of mood. They were happy. The rest of the day, indeed the next week, passed without incident or hospitalizations. Things went as quietly and as smoothly as they ever do in the largest homeless shelter in New York City.

I was outraged, and puzzled. A few weeks later, I decided to write a questionnaire asking the clients about their feelings about September 11. The results confirmed the same difference. Only one client had incorporated the events of 9-11 into his psychotic thinking. In an interview, he told me that he was an army general, that he owned the World Trade towers and had lost a lot of money in the deal, and that in the last few days he had been back and forth to Afghanistan to negotiate reparations. He seemed quite happy about it all, though. There was almost a twinkle in his eye as he told me this. I wondered if he was pulling my leg. Another client, in response to each question on my form, had written in large letters: FUCK IT, FUCK IT, FUCK IT. The vast majority of the clients wrote about 9-11 as something they felt bad about, but it wasn't much more than a blip on their daily consciousness. (To be fair, though, there was some fallout later in the fall of 2002. When the United States began bombing Afghanistan in October, a number of clients became unstable and were hospitalized.)

I read over my surveys. I puzzled over the clients' bizarre stability, their incredible lightness of mood right after the attacks. And then I realized that on that day only, the world's trauma matched their own. They live out the violence and despair and bloodiness and trauma of 9-11 every day, and it was an enormous relief that for one or two days the world experienced that same level of trauma. They weren't alone anymore, and they felt good and . . . normal. For once, everybody else felt like them. That's what mental illness does to you.

It made me realize that while I have traveled in the same country my clients live in, they live in that country all the time. I am familiar with, but not an occupant of, the poisonous terrain they inhabit on a permanent basis.

⚬ ⚬ ⚬

So this is what I've learned about serious mental illness in my strange odyssey: *It is so awful that it's like living September 11 every day of your life.*

Or to put it another way: Even when America was attacked, it meant nothing to their mental interiors.

epilogue

Boontan Wasn't Here

> Think no more; 'tis only thinking
> Lays lads underground.

A. E. HOUSMAN, *A Shropshire Lad*

New Haven, Connecticut, is regarded by most people familiar with it as a troubled and downscale city, encumbered with an unusual number of severe urban problems—poverty, violence, drugs, disease—for a city of its relatively modest size. While I recognize these assessments to be essentially true, that is not the way that I have come to regard New Haven. To me, New Haven is idyllic, sylvan, and pastoral, something closer to an old and sleepy European village than a contemporary American city. I look at the Green, and where most people see a tattered city park littered with garbage, I see a serene meadow. I look at the housing projects, and I see mansions. I visit the psychiatric units of New Haven's large hospitals, which I do often to recruit patients in my new life as a researcher and writer in the Yale Department of Psychiatry, and I feel like I am on the sundeck of a cruise ship.

I am fully aware that my vision is biased and off-kilter. I realize that I have spent too much time around black chairs, and I know that what I see is warped. But it is simply the case that everybody and everything around me, no matter how tense and harried they can become, remain to me unaccountably wonderful and sedate.

You see, about a year ago I decided to forgo black chairs. I'm not sure how to explain it other than to say that my wife got pregnant, and after the enormity of this sunk in, it led to a grand reassessment of our lives. In particular, my wife and I reexamined my penchant for spending thirteen hours a day in shelters for very little money.

To put it simply, I decided to settle down. To the great relief of my family, impending fatherhood made me more bourgeois almost overnight, and Laura and I did what generations of New Yorkers have done before us when faced with the imminent arrival of children: we moved to Connecticut. Oddly, the people in the psychiatry department at Yale were intrigued by my experience with black chairs and hired me in a week.

So these days I mainly sit at a desk in a quiet office on the edge of an Ivy League campus and analyze data for a study about how best to get people with psychosis and substance abuse into psychiatric treatment. I like my work. Things have come full circle; I seem to have combined the two halves of my life, Ivy League institutions and work with psychiatric patients, into something whole and lasting. My parents have a newfound respect for what I've been up to all these years. And besides, I think the research is important. The importance of getting into psychiatric treatment is something I have learned to value over the years.

Our baby, Louis, was born a few months after we moved to Connecticut. He was born in December, on a day when it was seventy degrees. It was like that for the rest of the week, and there were reports in the paper about global warming and how Connecticut's climate was going to be like Florida's within fifty years. I found the climatic change surrounding Louis's birth appropriate, because my world has changed forever too. From birth Louis had extraordinarily refined features and the most beautifully shaped head crowned with fine brown hair. He is an exact combination of Laura and me—which we thought would be unsightly, since we're so different—but it turns out Louis is quite a looker, with flirtatious long eyebrows. Not only do Laura and I agree that he is the most irrepressibly charming and funny baby the world has ever seen, he keeps me completely on my toes.

Under my newfound domestic circumstances, there is no longer much time for obsessive thought! He wakes me at six and demands milk. "Daddy! Daddy!!" he calls from the crib. I feed him and watch him suck on his bottle, the nipple almost glowing in the morning light, and I know that I am a changed man, a man in love. Laura comes down a little bit later for coffee, which I like to make for her, and the three of us eat pancakes together. I look at the clock—it is now six thirty—and I think how pathetic it was that I spent so many years sleeping as late as I could, essentially to avoid being awake. Louis cries again, and I dismiss these reveries and get back to feeding him. He has a way of making the things of this world enormously clear. Even more than Prozac does.

◦ ◦ ◦

Recently, when visiting my parents in Cold River, I came across, in the bottom of a drawer in my old desk, a short story I wrote eighteen years ago, inspired by our (Henry's and Nick's and my) numerous trips to the 7-11. While I was the one to actually write it down, Nick, Henry and I all came up with the ideas together.

DAIRY MART

By Charles Barber and Henry Court and Nick Lanzetti

Bob and I were drinking coffee, as usual, after another hard day at the brick factory, when Nancy, our waitress, came to tell us the bad news. In her lovely pink uniform, she sidled up to the counter and said that she and the donut-maker had just been listening to the radio in the back, and sure enough the day had finally arrived. Reagan and Gorbachev were about to push the button. "Yup," she said, "the apocalypse is indeed near. Would you like a little more coffee to go with your Boston Cremes?" "Surely," we said. Now Bob and I could have gone to listen to the radio ourselves to confirm the news, but we trusted Nancy: she'd always given us good service.

As other customers shrieked and ran for their cars Bob and I looked each other in the eye knowingly. We took a final swig of our coffee, ate the last of the Boston Cremes and tipped Nancy generously for everything she'd done. Yup, I thought as we slowly walked to the parking lot, the day had come. Now you might have thought we would be panicked, but we weren't put out in the slightest. This was a day we had long prepared for. We knew exactly what to do. There was almost excitement in my heart as we got into Bob's old car and drove out old Route Nine. There were jackknifed trucks and crazily speeding vehicles and people hyperventilating and vomiting as they sat in their cars pulled over at the side of the road. But Bob and I ignored it all and headed slowly, even calmly, the five miles out Route Nine to the Dairy Mart.

"Coffee's Ready . . . Freedom's Waiting." It had been that slogan, appearing in great green and red letters on an enormous banner sailing above the store that had first attracted Bob and me to the Dairy Mart. The Mart, as we came to call it, is just a few blocks from the brick factory where we used to work. To think, for years we drove by the mart every day, without even stopping! It's amazing the treasures that lie right in front of people that they never notice! But on that day, I'd say it was about a year ago, when I first noticed the banner, I just knew that we had to go in. The slogan beckoned me. It was really something I had no control over, like the pull of some super-powered magnetic field. The banner was right of course—there was both coffee and freedom to be found there. Coffee and freedom like you wouldn't believe.

When we walked into the Dairy Mart, we just couldn't believe what we saw. Everything could be found there! Somehow, I guess being so busy at the brick factory, I had missed the whole convenience store phenomenon. When I was growing up there was the neighborhood store, where if you had to, you could get a loaf of bread and some milk and soda. But here in front of us was an entire universe filled with magazines and books and video games, and cereal, milk, orange juice, dog food, and toilet paper; and hot dog carousels and beef jerky and 48 ounce sodas; and ice cream and canned corn and tacos with all the fixings. Coffee and freedom were the least of it! It was dazzling. That first day, we must have spent a couple of hours playing video games, reading a few newspapers, and eating a meatball hero or two. No one hurried us to leave. The manager, Bert, even let us stand behind the counter where the lottery tickets and dirty magazines were sold and introduced us to the regulars: Sharon, a taxi driver, Susan, a lawyer, and Harry, an engineer. All of them were real smart and friendly. We had such a great time we came back that same night; after a while it got so Bob and I started going to the Dairy Mart like twice a day, during lunch, after work, you name it, whenever we could.

Now I want to say right here that Bob and I did go to college for a few years, but we both got sick and tired of it and dropped out on the same day. College just seemed to be about fancy jargon—finding different terminology to say just basic things. So together we got work at the brick factory—they were the only ones who were hiring. It started out as just a job, but we grew to truly love brick making. Over time we found that there was something magical about shaping molten elements into beautiful neat rectangular shapes. People don't realize this, but there are a lot of different types of bricks out there.

But perhaps because we had that sort of frustrated intellectual side, Bob and I spent a lot of time reading at the Dairy Mart. Actually it was when I was reading "Time" at the Mart that I had the great brainstorm. There was a cover article about Reagan's great nuclear build-up. There was a lot of analysis of all the new warheads, and there was a picture of the old fall-out shelters from the Sputnik era. There was a graph showing the exponential growth of nuclear weapons in America. In a later section of the magazine, in the business section, there was an article about the exploding number of convenience stores in the country. The graph looked extremely similar to that detailing warheads. Now this is when it occurred to me: I thought, hold on, now, maybe the proliferation of Dairy Marts and the nuclear build-up were somehow related! What if . . . yes! . . . what if the Dairy Marts were like . . . yes! . . . the new fall-out shelter for the Eighties? Crazy, I thought. Looking at the dingy old fall-out shelters, I thought how could they have anything to do with the magical Technicolor high-tech world that I found myself in now? But then again standards do change and the Dairy Marts did have all the modern conveniences that might keep people alive for (gasp!) years—they were, yes, they were fully equipped fall-out shelters! And, then I thought, due to the population explosion, they would need to be self-selecting. It wasn't like the Fifties; not everybody could get in. There wouldn't be enough room! Only those perspicacious enough, or patriotic enough, with the verve and imagination to respond to banners like "Coffee's Ready . . . Freedom's Waiting," only these people would be able to access the Fall-out Shelters of the Eighties. It was like Darwinian or something—only those with special skills would survive, and go on to produce the next race.

With a gleam in my eye, I excitedly told my theory to Bob on the way back to the brickyard.

"I don't think so," he said.

"Come on!" I said. "Look at the green and red fake plastic brick they're made out of! That's like a nuclear Teflon! It has to be!" I said. "And furthermore, did you ever notice how small the windows are! I looked and I think there are power blinds that can roll down to cover them. That's so as to provide protection in the event of a nuclear incident."

"That's hard to believe," Bob said.

Just to be sure, I went by myself late one night to the Dairy Mart, and took a sample of that green and red material that the building was made of. The material was so strong that it took a long time to cut even a tiny amount of the material away. Later, at the brickyard, I snuck into the chief engineer's office to identify the sample. After hours of sophisticated scientific research I identified it as SuperHiDensity ThermoDuroBlast Brick, the most expensive on the market. The executives at the Dairy Mart Corporation and the higher-ups in the Defense Department (for clearly they were related) had to be concerned about protecting against bombs, or there was no way they would get a brick that expensive. We didn't even carry them in the brickyard.

As I operated the brick machine the next day, I experienced a vision. I saw the hundreds of bricks in front of me transform magically into a hundred little Dairy Marts, each perfect replicas of the real thing with the exact green and red colors and the coffee and freedom banners. It lasted for a few minutes and then the hundred little Dairy Marts transformed back into bricks.

Bob had been skeptical, but when I told him about the expensive bricks and the vision, he finally agreed with me. "You're right," he said. "There's no way they would get a hold of those SuperHiDensityThermoDuroBlast Bricks if they didn't have something up their sleeves," he said.

So from then on, it was just a matter of waiting. Sure, we went there and drank sodas and played video games like all the other customers, but really we were just waiting for the day the bomb dropped and we could capitalize on our discovery. Bob and I both noticed that on our many return visits to the Dairy Mart Burt and Sharon and Susan and Harry all looked at us with a special gleam in their eye. They knew they'd be spending the rest of their lives with us. We were in.

So on the day the bomb was going to drop, Bob and I pulled off to Route Nine and up to the Dairy Mart. There was Burt standing outside, welcoming us.

"Hurry!" he said. "They're just about to drop it!"

"You see," I told Bob, smiling. Bob beamed back at me.

We sprinted inside the Dairy Mart. Sharon was there, placing hot dogs on the carousel, and Harry and Susan, eating beef jerky. We were all in a great mood. It was a little party, just for the elite.

"Where the hell have you guys been? We've been expecting you!" they said, hugging us.

At that moment, we heard the largest explosion ever. The whole building rocked. Exactly on cue, the power blinds went down. All of us rushed to the window just in time to see the mushroom cloud going up. It was a lovely, lovely sight.

It's the first story I wrote. I don't know if it's literature, but it completely reflects the surrealism of the world we lived in. If nothing else, it proves that we lived in some mental place that bordered on the psychotic. But it's like everything else about our lives back then: nothing ever came of it. The story sat in a drawer for eighteen years.

᭜ ᭜ ᭜

It turns out Boontan wasn't here.

At a writer's conference I attended last summer, I read aloud the earlier passage about Henry's trashing of his dorm room and his penchant for writing "Boontan Was Here" in the Wilson bathrooms.

After I finished, a young woman, slightly flushed, approached me.

"Did you really use the quote 'Boontan was here'?" she asked.

"Yes," I said.

"I can't believe it," she said.

She had recently graduated from Wilson. In her senior year, she explained, there had been a great controversy over Boontan. Apparently, in the years after Henry died, the Boontan cartoon had taken hold on campus. Generations of students had taken to drawing it in the bathrooms and the underground tunnels at the college. So much so, that seventeen years later, Boontan was scrawled everywhere and had become a kind of symbol of . . . well, nobody knew quite what.

"And last spring, it just erupted," the woman said. "There was an article on the front page of the college newspaper proclaiming that Boontan was racist and sexist."

"In what way?" I said.

"Well, you know, the eyes in the drawing are kind of slanty, and people thought it was making fun of Asian people. And Boontan sounds kind of like, um, poontang. Some people thought Boontan dated back to the sixties, and was maybe meant to show support for the Vietnam War, or was an attack on the Vietnamese people or something. An editorial in the paper called for the removal of Boontans all over campus."

In the days that followed, some students removed or painted over the graffiti, while others — no doubt spiritual descendants of Henry — drew Boontan back again on various surfaces in the late night hours, under cover of darkness. In the end, while his numbers surely decreased, Boontan survived. I am happy to report that they couldn't destroy him.

"Thank you," I said to the woman, rather incredulously. It was difficult to conceive that Henry could have influenced other people — that he actually had followers was absolutely unbelievable — but I could think of no better tribute to the legacy of Henry Court. He would have loved it, certainly much more than the Henry S. Court scholarship for promising nerds that his mother had created. I told Nick, back in his dark lair in the basement of his parent's home, about the battle for political correctness that Henry had set off. He laughed and laughed. For us, it felt like a kind of victory.

All along, ever since that first session in the lair, I had been asking Nick if he knew the origin of Henry's Boontan obsession. He tried, but he couldn't remember anything about it. But this story seemed to jostle some deeply hidden memory.

"Yes, yes, I remember now! Yes . . . at our freshman orientation, there was a guy called John Boontan who never showed up. At the first reception, they had out on a table those name tags they always have for all the new students. You were supposed to put them on your shirt or sweater or whatever. At the end there was only one left on the table, and it said, "Hello, My Name is . . . John Boontan." Henry picked it up—you know how he was always picking up things and collecting them—and put it on the wall in his room. And somehow that turned into the basis for the graffiti."

"And John Boontan never showed up?" I said.

"No," Nick said, "he never did."

Or, then again, maybe Boontan is here. On a flight to London, Laura and I noticed the nametag of the stewardess. "Mary Boontan," it read.

✤ ✤ ✤

Even though I had taken classes, in a desultory fashion, for only a few semesters, Wilson duly sends me the alumni directory, the college magazine, and fund-raising solicitations. Strangely enough, Henry Court is listed in the alumni directory as a proud member of the class of 1984. His entry looks disturbingly normal until you spot the requisite asterisk next to his name—Henry of course was the sort of person who seemed to attract asterisks. I looked for the code at the bottom of the page, assuming that it indicated that the person was deceased. But no, being dead was represented by two asterisks. One asterisk meant merely that the person's address was unknown. Henry Court, Address Unknown: confounding officialdom to the end.

I was just about to toss a recent issue of the college magazine when I noticed that it included an article about William Court in his retirement. In the piece there was a picture of William from the 1970s, teaching a small seminar. He looked remarkably like Henry. At long last, the elusive image of Henry's face had come to me! I poured over the picture and absorbed it into my mind. The empty cloud with which I had always pictured Henry was filled in by Mr. Court's strong features! But there was a major difference, I noticed. There was a happiness and simplicity to the picture of Mr. Court, who was smiling as he made some presumably profound point to his group of students. As much as I tried, I couldn't connect that mixture of peacefulness and potency with anything having to do with Henry. In the article there were comments from people in his field saying that Mr. Court had been way before his time, and that he had identified the need for examining literature in its cultural context twenty or thirty years before it became fashionable to do so. There was little of William's personal life in the profile, certainly nothing of Joyce and Henry, but it did mention that he had suffered a mild stroke, from which he was recovering nicely, and was happily remarried and living at a farmhouse in the Berkshires . . .

Living at a farm in the Berkshires? What? Why? It had to be the same place. Why would he do that? Why the hell would he choose to live with the ghosts of his family?

I got up the nerve to call him a few months later. I was progressing with this memoir, and it had been my intention all along to contact William at a certain point to tell him that I was writing about his son and his family. I wasn't asking for his approval exactly, but I wanted him to know and I wanted him to read what I had written.

Sure enough, he was at the farm. He answered on the second ring. He sounded alert and strong. I asked about his health.

"Oh, I'm doing fine, really. I do have to take naps in the afternoons, something I never used to do," he said laughing.

We caught up for a while, and then I told him about my writing. He didn't seem at all put off, or surprised, or intruded upon. "I would like to see some of it," he said.

᭟ ᭟ ᭟

We arranged to meet a few weeks later in New York, to coincide with a trip that William and his new wife were planning to visit her daughter and family. When Mr. Court opened the door to the apartment, I noticed the usual signs of aging: the hair thinner, the middle wider, the lines on the face deeper. But essentially he was the same. It was hard to believe that he'd had a stroke. We shook hands warmly. He introduced his new wife, his new son-in-law, his new granddaughter. We all had coffee in a sun-lit living room. Mr. Court and I chatted as the little girl, about seven, danced and played around us. His wife Sara was energetic, like Joyce, but calm. I could tell that she must have been strikingly pretty when she was younger. "We were sweethearts in college," William said almost bashfully. "We almost got married back then." I couldn't help but think about all that would have been avoided if they had.

After coffee, William and I went for a walk in Riverside Park. It was a bright morning and there were kids, joggers, and dogs everywhere. William walked quickly. I told him about my work with psychiatric patients at the shelter. He seemed really interested in what I was doing and asked a lot of questions about it. "That's dynamite," I remember he said.

There was a break in the conversation. We were standing near the Hudson. "Do you think about Henry a lot?" I said.

"Oh, yeah," William replied. "Pretty much every day. But, you know, it's usually not in a tragic way. I'll think about some little thing we did together or some place we went. I dream about him a lot too," he said.

So do I, I thought.

"I remember one time, he must have been nineteen, I told him he was drinking too much. Of course we were both drinking beer at the time," he smiled. "I told him he needed to lay off the sauce. It was late at night, and he started to wrestle with me. It started off as just playing around, but then it got sort of serious. He pinned me. I was surprised at his strength. We started laughing, and then he said he loved me."

He was sort of looking beyond me, out toward the river. The sun played on the water. "You know, people of my generation—and I think your father is the same way—we didn't say stuff like that. Don't express your emotions, stiff upper lip, and all that. Henry was trying to be different," he said.

It may have been the glint on the sun, but I thought I saw a tear appear in his eye. But then it disappeared, if it had ever been there at all.

We went to a Chinese restaurant for lunch. Mr. Court told me about the writing he was doing in retirement, and the work he liked to do outside on the farm.

Finally, I had to ask him. "Why do you live there?" I said.

"Good question," he said, completely unfazed. "I bought the place in the sixties, you know. I lived there for a long time before . . . and it was always much more my place than anybody else's. Henry and Joyce didn't go there much . . ."

Except to commit suicide, I thought.

"I don't know," he said. "When I drive up the driveway, I don't think this is where my family died. I just don't think it. It may be strange, but I just don't."

I very much wanted to find this perverse, but I wasn't able to.

We paid the bill and walked outside. When I left him, we were in front of a small political bookstore, off Broadway. It was, Mr. Court explained, one of the few lefty bookstores still around.

"It's my son-in-law's birthday tomorrow. I wanted to get him something," he said. He held out his hand. "Great to see you, Charlie."

"And you too," I said. I handed him a packet of my writings about Henry. We shook hands, and then, I think, we hugged.

Before I went back to Broadway I looked around just in time to see him entering the bookstore. I shook my head. I was amazed and slightly confounded by his ability to block out the past. I have learned to compartmentalize things, but nothing like the way he had been able to do. For better or worse, he was the master.

What a wonderful, miraculous, extraordinary thing stability is, it doesn't matter how you get there, I thought as I headed home to Connecticut.

A week later I got a letter from Mr. Court. He had read my writing, he liked it, and he gave me permission to write this story however I wanted.

◦ ◦ ◦

Nick never became the writer or professor that he had planned on being in high school. His career of choice was that of a (failed) childcare worker. He never married the love of his life, since she, for reasons I never quite discovered, broke off the engagement; he continued to live with his parents, gained more and more weight, ate a lot junk food, underwent bouts of smoking and drinking heavily, and went through about a dozen girlfriends, almost all of whom could uncharitably be described (and were by me) as "airheads." He spoke to them in a language they couldn't understand; most could not tolerate the amount of deep mystification that came with being with Nick and quickly left. He worked for fourteen years as a childcare worker, gaining some seniority and pension money, only to be fired after he punched a coworker who had started seeing a woman he was going out with. He was unemployed for a year and spent most of it in the lair, avoiding sunlight and contact with as many people as he could.

In an earlier draft, I had written about Nick: "He continues to stagnate. In high school he wanted to be a big-time journalist or novelist. Now he spends most of his time driving in circles and watching movies he's seen a dozen times before."

Nick responded, "It's true enough, but you haven't got it quite right. I think I can do better. I'll write you with, let's say, a fuller characterization."

His letter arrived a week later.

Dear Charlie,

What can you say about my wayward life of the past 18 years? If you wished to be brief, you might say something like:

Nick's immense academic promise would, in retrospect, become inversely proportional to the success of his later endeavors. He quit his job after working 14 years in a menial position at a social service agency when he got into a scuffle with another worker. I believe it was all over a woman.

Or, if you wanted to provide a more detailed account, you could say:

If Charlie and Henry lived in their heads too much, Nick would dwell in his head to an even greater extent during his own middle years. Bits and pieces of the novels and songs and the philosophies he had known in his earlier life floated in suspension about his skull and applied themselves at times with full force to his perceptions of the world at large. As such, reality often became an afterthought of sorts, and was useful only as a backdrop against which his private epic novel was set.

Or, you could write:

Henry was as passive-aggressive as Nick was not. While Henry never took his rage out on others, the same could not be said of Nick, especially in the years after Henry's death. Perhaps there was some sort of strange over-compensatory effect at work in

Nick's psyche, which demanded now, in private memoriam to his dead pal, that all wrongs be exposed as wrongs, no matter how trivial, and that all wrongs be outlined and redressed, if not always with fisticuffs, then at the very least with a verbal tirade or two. Likewise, he would love hard and fast and desperately, and would often be given over to fits of grandiose romanticism, which when they passed, would leave him depressed and despondent.

Or:

Nick lived a disjointed life, and often fancied himself a professional underachiever and dilettante. He was eclectic to be sure, but he tended to practice an eclecticism of the absurd, whereby in one month he read Pynchon or Plato or Proust, and then in the next month, chase after barefoot tanned women in beachside bars. He yearned to be entertained, and so the actual source of the entertainment mattered little. A dead author or live sex goddess would do just as well. Through his twenties and thirties he successfully avoided most adult middle-class responsibilities, and by 35, he determined he would not have children of his own. "The line stops here" he would declare, relieved and rueful at once.

Or:

Though Nick fancied himself a cosmopolitan in theory, he was provincial in practice. While fairly well traveled intellectually, he limited himself geographically to a few square miles of land around Cold River. If he took a map and marked his boyhood area with an "X" and then drew a small circle around the "X" he would describe an area saturated with the major events of his life. As he drove through Cold River, this sense of existential density made his head spin. He would say to himself: This is where I kissed her; and this is where the cops came for us; this is where we first made love; this is where I studied books; this is where I laughed aloud; this is where she lives now; and this is where he is laid to rest. He wondered how many other lives lay throbbing within this very same circle and whether one day the force of all the memories and ghosts within the circle would cause it to burst and scatter its contents across the earth, and whether such a random dispersal would in the end bring him and the others a measure of Peace,

Nick

I read the letter, and wanted to cry.

⋄ ⋄ ⋄

My brother Tom, the doctor, had dinner with Nick and me not so long ago. We had a great time, and Nick was as funny and irreverent as ever. Afterward Tom said, "I think he's clinically depressed." It had never even occurred to me to think of Nick in that way. My initial and therefore dominant impression of him was as a gifted and industrious student, with ambitions in the world; and despite fourteen years of evidence to the contrary, I always thought of him as the most stable of the three of us. Even if it was taking him some time, he was still destined to do, or to write, something brilliant and indelible, like the great tragicomic absurdist novel of our generation. But when Tom made his informal diagnosis, it made perfect sense.

In his lair I haltingly asked Nick if he felt he might be depressed.

"Oh yeah, of course I am," he said.

"Have you ever gotten any treatment?" I asked.

"Oh shit yeah, I've seen a bunch of psychologists and psychiatrists," he said.

"Did any of them treat you with medications?" I said.

"Oh sure," he said. "I've taken Zoloft, Paxil, Prozac, you name it. I've taken a ton of them. None of them had any effect on me whatsoever."

So this has been the story of not two but three sons of Cold River who have been touched by various forms of mental illness. Henry was no doubt severely depressed, and drug addicted, and probably psychotic. And now Nick was seriously depressed, too. Worse off than me. No wonder we all got along so well together—we all carried the same seeds of future disturbance.

"So what have you been up to?" I asked Nick when he called the other day. He sounded a little drunk.

"Well, if you really want to know, I've been conducting an experiment. For the last three weeks I've been listening intently to the Rolling

Stones albums *Sticky Fingers* and *Let It Bleed* alternately. I've been trying to figure out which is the better record. I listen to one of them each day while I'm driving around. So far I'm leaning toward *Let It Bleed*."

"Oh, I always liked *Sticky Fingers*," I said.

"But *Let It Bleed* is more versatile. You can do more things listening to it, I think."

"Have you heard Mick's yelp on *Sticky Fingers*?"

"What yelp?" Nick said, suddenly perking up.

"It's about two thirds of the way through 'Can't You Hear Me Knocking,'" I explained. "Mick spontaneously emits a joyous cry during Mick Taylor's guitar solo. It's hard to hear, you have to really listen for it. It's kind of buried in the mix about two-thirds of the way through."

"Oh wow, I'll listen for it," Nick said, almost excited. "Thanks a lot." It seemed likely that right after we hung up, Nick was going to run for his stereo to search for the buried yelp in "Can't You Hear Me Knocking." He seemed almost grateful that I'd given him something to do for the evening.

"And how much longer will the experiment go on?" I asked.

"I think another month or so. I think I'll probably have an answer for you then."

"Will you call me when the results are in?" I said.

"Definitely," Nick said. "I'll listen for the yelp."

⋄ ⋄ ⋄

A few years ago I ran into Ruby, my Jamaican compatriot at the group home, at a video store. I was pleased and heartened to see that she was selecting a bunch of violent movies to take home. She looked just the same.

"How's the group home?" I said.

"Good," she said.

"And how are the guys?"

"Eddie, Jaime, they good. Eddie settled down a lot. They put him on some new meds, he doesn't bite anybody anymore. And Jaime, you know him, he's a good man."

"And Luke?"

A strange look came across her face.

"Luke?" she said. "Oh. He died. He had one of them seizures in the middle of the night, and he just died. Oh, that was years ago."

I don't remember saying good-bye to Ruby, but I do remember leaving the video store crying. The poor bloody soul, what a life. So those lips turned blue after all. That would-be intelligent face was gone. What a wretched life he had! The poor miserable son of a bitch. I drove around for an hour thinking about him, and crying for him, and eventually feeling angry at . . . I didn't know whom to blame. It made me feel depleted and wretched and hopeless about the world. There was no point to anything when someone like Luke could be maimed before he even entered the world and then, equally arbitrarily and horribly, dismissed from it.

Isn't that strange? I cried for Luke, and I never cried for Henry.

⋅❖⋅ ⋅❖⋅ ⋅❖⋅

Obsessiveness, it turns out, may have its advantages.

According to Dr. Jerome Groopman, writing in *The New Yorker*:

Recent studies indicate that people with OCD have distinctive neurological circuitry. These differences are most pronounced in the limbic lobe, the caudate nucleus, and the orbital front cortex, the areas of the brain which participate in anxiety and automatic responses. Sophisticated brain scans show that when a potentially distressing scenario is confronted by a person without OCD, the brain activity in these areas barely registers on the screen; in a person with OCD, however, there is an intense and prolonged firing of neurons, and the scans light up like a Christmas tree.

According to Groopman's article, the director of the neuropsychology program at Boston Children's Hospital, Dr. Jane Holmes Bernstein, suggests that OCD is a response to excess arousal—arousal in this instance meaning a neurological response to environmental stimuli. "[Holmes Bernstein] pointed to the recent studies . . . which show that, under certain conditions, people with OCD make associations between neutral as well as aversive stimuli more quickly than people without OCD. Holmes Bernstein believes that both this high state of arousal and the anxiety it produces may have evolutionary roots. In a prehistoric environment, those with the ability to focus and lock on to stimuli — particularly threatening elements in the environment — could have been better suited to escape the dangers of predators and treacherous terrain."

There has been further theorizing in psychiatric journals. If the higher levels of arousal of people with OCD was once an environmentally advantageous characteristic, this condition may have outgrown its usefulness in the modern and arguably calmer world. Since people no longer need to be quite so vigilant to the dangers of the physical world, the excess levels of arousal turn elsewhere, to repetitive thoughts and worries.

I wonder. Could William and Robert have been the sole survivors of the shipwreck because the neurological circuitry of their limbic systems made them more aroused, more aware, and more responsive to their environment? Did they in fact have OCD, or pre-OCD? Have I inherited their neurological circuitry? Am I lucky to have inherited it? Or is this all just a simple, cheap explanation of complicated events and feelings? Or is it all just an excuse, a bullshit excuse for privileged white people like me to not take responsibility for their problems?

Such are the mysteries of one's family's neurology.

⚬ ⚬ ⚬

I have but one insight about the three of us. Henry, Nick, and I: we thought too much. Way too much. Lacking a real war, ideas were what we made war with.

For the three of us, ideas were reality. Thinking something made it unquestionably real. We lived out Shakespeare's dictum "Nothing is good or bad but thinking makes it so." Just as Henry's father no longer taught English literature but instead analyzed how English literature was taught, we three lived in a world removed multiple levels from reality. Our world was ideas about ideas about ideas. I am positive, as positive as I am about anything concerning Henry, that he really lived in the malevolent and horrific world he created in his mind, just as I thought I had perpetuated violent acts simply because I conceived of them. And Nick fully lives his private epic novel, a novel that never reaches the pages, and perhaps never will.

Our parents and grandparents had been workers, manufacturers, and farmers. Henry's parents and mine were intellectuals, people who manipulated symbols for a living. That was the trick that my father and Mr. Court had mastered, and that Henry and I just didn't get. Our parents were able to play with ideas—in fact, make a nice career out of playing with ideas—whereas Henry and I actually believed them, and lived them, and took on all their monstrous potentiality. But unlike our parents, we never wrote or produced anything with our supposed insights. Although as I think about it, Henry was, in his own way (as when he kept the door open so others could view the trashings), a would-be performance artist.

This is what I have come to believe: everybody has to have their war (or at least everybody male). If a real war is not readily available, then you create one yourself. My ancestors William and Joseph had their war with the sea and the elements on the shores of Massachusetts; my father had World War II; Mr. Court had Vietnam and its domestic aftermath; Mrs. Court had a war with alcohol and depression and the death of her son; Michael Jasny had a war with his own warped and overactive mind; Luke had a war with seizures. But Henry and I, we had to make it all up. There was no war, really, no true war. We were smart, privileged, funny, healthy, reasonably athletic, and good-looking. We came from nice homes and all that. Nothing to complain about. So, in search of conflict, we made up the war with the trees, the war within. No, it's not quite that I created OCD for myself—or that Henry created his own depression and alcoholism or whatever accounted for his extreme misery—but the fact was that this turmoil was in many ways more interesting than peace (every unhappy family is unhappy in its own way; every family is happy in its own way, and all that). All of this contributed to the appeal of the madness that took over Henry and me for a while.

But even in the worst of it, there was one thing that always separated me from Henry: even at the depth of my confusion, I thought the world was beautiful. Part of my frustration when I felt homicidal in Harvard Yard was that I was unable to do what I always wanted to do—travel, write, dance, meet A. S. Byatt, go to Paris, get sunburned, anything, even when I was in such a state that I wasn't even able to take a walk outside. It seemed to me back then, and often now, that the world was extreme and divergent, terrible and beautiful at the same time. A terrible beauty. An exquisite horror. A pretty wreck. Wonderful and horrible, simultaneously. Sometimes these days another repetition of words goes through my brain:

Wonderful horrible wonderful horrible wonderful horrible wonderful horrible Wonderful horrible wonderful horrible wonderful horrible wonderful horrible Wonderful horrible wonderful horrible wonderful horrible wonderful horrible wonderful horrible . . .

I like wonderful horrible better than black black black black black black black. I believe it is a more realistic, accurate accounting of the world and better represents my state of mind. For sure, I have dark obsessive disturbing thoughts that sometimes seem to spill over into reality. Things can still be apocalyptic; there are even still the occasional moments when I don't know if I'll make it through, when my body feels whipped and I stumble through the world and all its bareness. But those days are rare.

I have learned, through hard and painful experience, that ideas mean nothing unless attached to action. I lost that awareness for a good ten years of my life and have had to relearn it, and most days—not every day, but most days—it saves me from oblivion.

I live not in blackness but in a pale light. It is light but pale; pale, yet light.

⭑ ⭑ ⭑

As I have written, Laura has never been the least bit indulgent about my OCD. She is matter-of-fact about my bad thoughts or "negative thinking," as we have come to call my now usually only passing afflictions.

Laura is direct. She says exactly what's on her mind. She doesn't even need to speak it usually; her face registers her joy, warmth, anger, pain, or whatever it is she's feeling. She is overt in her emotions; there is no filtering. Often I find Laura's emoting to be disconcerting. I get upset when she raises her voice or slams a door. "This is not something that one does," is the prescribed thought that automatically runs through my mind.

When I am overwhelmed with negative thoughts, Laura comforts and soothes me. We try to push them aside together. We try not to waste much time on them. These days we don't talk about them often, maybe three times a year. Instead of talking, we do things together, purposeful things. Now I try to channel my abstracted apocalyptic energy into producing things, like writing or washing socks. Having clean socks seems about as important as anything else these days.

It reminds me of one of my clients. Terry had schizophrenia and was homeless for many years. When he lived in the subway, he heard the whispering voices of the other passengers all day long, telling him he was horrible, pathetic, a bum, a psycho, dirty, smelly. These voices would build into a mad crescendo and eventually turn into something angrier and more malevolent, provoking his out-of-control, full-blown psychotic episodes. Years later, when he moved into a community residence, he became obsessed with acquiring as many shirts (nice, button-down Oxford shirts) as he could. His goal was to accumulate a hundred shirts. He asked me daily for shirts. He asked if he could buy my old shirts, and asked if he could buy the shirt I was wearing. Laura ended up buying shirts for him at church sales. Eventually he did reach his hundred shirts, and many more, the acquisition of which left him barely any space in his small, single room. He seemed content, if crowded. I regarded him as the Jay Gatsby of the community residence, with his hundreds and hundreds of shirts.

Terry wasn't normally assertive or nagging, and one day, annoyed, I asked him what was so damn important about having so many shirts.

"It's because every time I wear one, I feel a little better about myself. The more shirts I wear, the fewer voices I hear. The fewer voices I hear, the less likely I am to become psychotic. The shirts are armor against the voices. They're much stronger than the medicine you give me."

I'm no different from Terry, really: the more clean socks I wear, the more I write, and the more I get on with the business of actually doing things, the less obsessive and more functional I feel.

⚬ ⚬ ⚬

Laura and I invented something called the "Disclosure Act." Since I am still not skilled in speaking directly about things, every so often I write her a memo about my ruminations. I disclose everything, or almost everything. This memo writing is silly, we both know, and we laugh about it. Sometimes I think Henry and I would have benefited from a Disclosure Act of our own. Anything to break the almost universal male adolescent code of silence that we lived out. Anything to have broken the endless need for posturing, for "cool," for destructive silence.

Over the last twenty years, the most significant thing I have learned is this: if you slam doors now, you're less likely to kill yourself later.

᚛ ᚛ ᚛

Not long ago I asked my father after dinner what the worst decade of his life had been. I tend, in what I think is an artifact of OCD, to ask extreme and hypothetical kinds of questions—what was the best thing that ever happened to you, what was the worst thing, where would you travel if you could go anywhere for six months . . .

"Well, the 1940s, of course" my father said, "with the war." He paused for a moment. "But then again, as horrible as it was, at least things were clear and certain. And what about you?"

"Well, the early 1980s were pretty rough for me personally," I said.

"Why?"

"Well, it's when I first . . . had obsessive compulsive disorder." The words just came blurting out.

"First had what?" my father said. (I should note that while my parents were involved in referring me to the therapist in Cold River, the gory details of my diagnosis were always kept from them.)

My mother and father, who had been in a rather warm and friendly alcoholic mood, sat up and looked at me as if I was from another planet.

"Obsessive compulsive disorder," I said.

So began a long confession of my initial experiences with Prozac and with Dr. Porter and "negative thinking," and on and on. The whole wretched story. My parents had of course known something, in the most general way, about my difficulties (in my halting way, I had delivered various deeply veiled explanations of why I'd left Harvard), but they'd never heard from me or anyone else actual words or terms to describe it—and certainly not a medical diagnosis with symptoms and medications. My mother and father stopped drinking their white wine and gin, respectively, and listened very soberly for the next two and a half hours.

We happened to be listening to the Beatles' *White Album*. By coincidence (or perhaps not), at the very moment that I embarked on a specific explanation of OCD, the song "Revolution 9" was playing. "Revolution 9" is not a song at all but a soundscape created by John Lennon at his druggiest. So as I began to describe to my parents my murderous thoughts in Harvard Yard, a creepy English voice—an obsessive voice that I had fast forwarded through for years—repeated from the speaker behind me, ad infinitum, "Number nine, number nine, number nine, number nine, number nine, number nine." I kept on talking over the repeated numbers, but after a while I sensed that's what my narrative was starting to sound like to my parents. I couldn't help but smile: life and art conjoined again.

"Did you take drugs?" my mother interrupted in the middle of my story.

"No, I've told you a hundred times," I said. "I never took drugs."

She seemed almost disappointed, for the first time preferring drugs as a way of explaining my condition.

I described the worst times in Harvard Yard. "That year," my mother said, referring to my freshman year in college when I first cracked up, "there were so many things going on and I was just so busy that I wasn't able to notice what was going on with you." She started to cry.

I tried to explain to her that it really had nothing to do with my upbringing or anything she'd done, or hadn't done.

"Look, the Barbers are obsessive," I said. "Dad gets up in the middle of the night to write a few pages of his book because he can't get the thoughts out of his mind. I probably just got a little too much of it than is ideally good for me."

"But I don't understand," my mother said, "why it developed into a . . . medical condition."

"I don't know either," I said. "But it probably has something to do with neurons."

My mother didn't quite know what to make of this, and drank some more wine. After a while she turned to my father with a pained expression on her face. "Does this mean, Bill, that there's something wrong with our genes?"

My father considered this for a moment. "Not that we knew about—until now," he said, and looked accusingly—but also, I thought, lovingly—in my direction. My mother looked at me too, tears again welling in her eyes.

"Do you mean to tell me," my mother said, her voice quivering and her hand propelling the air downward with each word, as if trying to get up enough sheer physical momentum to say the words, "that you, Charlie, have a . . . mental illness?"

It was a good question. "No," I said, considering my words carefully. "I would say that I've been touched by mental illness." My mind flashed in the moment to Henry and Joyce and Karl and Michael Jasny: that was mental illness. I was not that. What I'd gone through, thankfully, was nothing compared to them—a drop versus an ocean.

But at the end of that difficult night, my father, at least, was relieved. "We always wondered what was going on during those years, when you sort of dropped out of things. It feels good to have an explanation." Even my mother thanked me. I still felt that she thought I was making half of it up, but right before I left, we all hugged and talked about how much we loved each other. My family never does that stuff.

Later that night, I felt nauseous lying in bed, trying to sleep. Laura was next to me. Louis was asleep in his room across the hall; I could hear his peaceful breathing on the baby monitor.

"I can't believe I told them," I said to her.

"It's good," she said. "It's about time they learned who their son really is . . . Not just the OCD part, but everything," she said.

"I feel liberated and sick all at the same time," I said to her.

"Of course," she said.

☙ ☙ ☙

"Why have you been writing about Henry?" my mother has said all along as I've written this account. "Why would you want to write about him? That was a long time ago, and he was just a mixed-up kid," she has said over and over again.

Exactly, I think. That's exactly why I'm writing about him.

A professor at graduate school, noting my seemingly gravitational pull toward "down and out," said that I had what the French call "a taste for mud." "I worried about you," he told me years later. "I wondered if you were just slumming it." But as I reach the conclusion of this manuscript—as I seem to have been able to put experience into a nice neat package, or seem to have made "order out of chaos, no more and no less" (to return to John Cheever's definition of literature)—I think I'm losing my taste for mud, and for Henry.

Mother, I don't think you need to be concerned now. I've written this account precisely to get rid of Henry. Now that I've put the story down, I'm quite sure I can let it go.

Henry's story is like a paper airplane that I've thrown off the span of the George Washington Bridge. It sails out into the air, through the green light, spiraling ever downward to the Hudson. The paper plane is just about to hit the water . . . and when it does, the story will be gone, Henry will have gone, Michael Jasny will have gone, all that will slowly, inexorably sink to the riverbed. I will have let them go.

And yet . . . maybe John Cheever was wrong. Try as I might, I can't quite seem to get rid of Henry. The plane sails always a few inches above the river. Always just above the surface. It never ever quite seems to hit the water. When I first started writing this account, I felt compelled to come up with a neat, succinct plot. After all, books have plots, don't they? A line or two, a small paragraph perhaps, that you can put on the jacket? But I could never come up with anything, just as I could never come up with a description of Henry's face.

But now, at the end, I think I've come upon the plot of this book:

⋆ ⋆ ⋆

Henry died, and I lived.

⋆ ⋆ ⋆

It's succinct enough, isn't it? Or, to put it another way:

This is has been a story about breathing in America—whether to, or not.

Breathing. You have to decide whether you are going to breathe or not. I remember after I dropped out of Harvard my mother and I were talking, in our roundabout way, about the difficulties that people have in the world. We happened to be listening to Miles Davis. "Look, living is hard," my mother said. "Breathing is hard. Just listen to the music." Indeed the pain that lay behind the exquisite and muted tones was obvious.

Henry decided not to breathe; Mrs. Court decided to join him in not breathing; Luke had no choice, and was not able to breathe; Mr.

Court decided to breathe; Michael Jasny went into the water, where he could not breathe; I chose to breathe . . .

Or:

Henry and Mrs. Court went up into the air; Michael Jasny went into water . . . and I—I stayed where I was.